Fundamental aspects of legal, ethical and professional issues in nursing

2nd Edition

Other titles in the series include

Fundamental Aspects of Long-Term Conditions
Fundamental Aspects of Palliative Care Nursing 2nd Edition
Fundamental Aspects of Research for Nurses
Fundamental Aspects of Finding Information
Fundamental Aspects of Infection Prevention and Control

Coming soon

Fundamental Aspects of Ophthalmic Nursing
Fundamental Aspects of Gastrointestinal Nursing

Series editor

Dr John Fowler

Note

Healthcare practice and knowledge are constantly changing and developing as new research and treatments, changes in procedures, drugs and equipment become available.

The author and publishers have, as far as is possible, taken care to confirm that the information complies with the latest standards of practice and legislation.

Fundamental aspects of legal, ethical and professional issues in nursing

2nd Edition

by

Sally Carvalho, Maggie Reeves and Jacquie Orford

Quay Books Division, MA Healthcare Ltd, St Jude's Church, Dulwich Road, London
SE24 0PB

British Library Cataloguing-in-Publication Data
A catalogue record is available for this book

© MA Healthcare Limited 2011
1st edition printed 2002
Reprinted 2007

ISBN-10: 1-85642-423-5
ISBN-13: 978-1-85642-423-3

Edited by Jessica Anderson

Cover design by Claire Majury
A & D Media Ltd, Wiltshire UK

Associate Publisher: Thu Nguyen

Printed by CLE, Huntingdon, Cambridgeshire

Contents

Foreword to the 1st Edition

We are going through a time of considerable change in the health service in this country, and there is an urgent need for all nurses to understand the professional implications of this. Some of the key issues emerging are of course closely linked to the National Health Service Plan, and the proposals for the future regulation of the healthcare professions.

The United Kingdom Central Council for Nursing, Midwifery and Health Visiting (UKCC), and the National Nursing Boards have disappeared and in their place is a new organisation with a new purpose and new ideas. Greater public involvement is starting to put the health professions under more scrutiny and pressure for improved quality in areas such as ethical and professional decision making and participation in services.

The Nursing and Midwifery Council (NMC) has taken over the future of regulation of nurses and midwives and is now the new body which is determined to reaffirm established standards and guidelines and to develop new ones.

Every nurse should not only be able to demonstrate that they have an awareness of the legislation and policy which is providing the future framework within which health care is delivered, but also that they should have a good grasp of the fundamental legal, ethical and professional aspects which are involved.

In order to accomplish this in the limited time often available for studying and keeping up-to-date, there is a need for both relevant and pertinent information to be easily available and accessible for nurses, as well as being presented clearly, concisely and precisely.

This excellent little book by Maggie Reeves and Jacquie Orford, sets out to accomplish an ideal introduction to the subject, and after reading through it, I am sure that you will be as convinced as I am that it achieves its aims.

Students on pre-registration nursing programmes will find this an essential book to guide them in their understanding of such issues as accountability, liability, truthfulness, truth-telling, choice, consent, autonomy, and advocacy.

Professor George Castledine

Foreword to the 2nd Edition

The publication of the 2nd edition this book has been timed to coincide with significant change in nursing and the wider healthcare context. The move towards an all graduate profession, and publication in 2010 of the new Nursing and Midwifery Council standards for pre-registration nursing, demonstrate a commitment to prepare nurses to provide care confidently in transformed health services and to meet changing patterns of healthcare need.

The population is undeniably living longer; healthcare must be able to provide for those who are critically ill, and for those who are increasingly old and living with long-term conditions who wish to be partners in their care and have their individual needs addressed in different ways. Graduate nurses are expected to demonstrate advanced knowledge and skills and to apply these competently to the planning and delivery of high quality care that is appropriate for the individual needs of each patient. However, it is not sufficient just to know 'how' to do something competently, the nurse must also know why. Nurses must be prepared to explain to others why they have taken a particular course of action. Most nursing activities are complex and involve making a number of judgements. In order to be able to make good decisions that will meet legal requirements, professional standards, and public expectations, the nurse must have a good understanding of the legal, ethical and professional context within which they work. The chapters of this book are designed to reflect the Nursing and Midwifery Council's four key competency domains of nursing: professional values; communication and interpersonal skills; nursing practice and decision-making; and leadership, management and team working.

This book provides readers with an introduction to the underpinning knowledge and values necessary to be a 'good' nurse. It provides an up-to-date legal framework for care and provides practical activities through which readers can explore professional issues and values and their application to practice. I believe this book will be useful both for those setting out on the pathway to be a nurse and for those who are more experienced who want to reflect on their care.

Jan Quallington
Associate Head Institute of Health and Society
University of Worcester

Acknowledgements

We would like to acknowledge the help of the many people who have assisted in the writing of this book.

Firstly, we thank the many students and colleagues with whom we have worked during our nursing and teaching careers. During this time, we have learnt how to answer questions and to find out answers, and to try to give these answers at the level the individual could understand. Students, in particular, have tested us to ensure that they have got the answer to their satisfaction and have challenged us with examples from clinical practice — some of which are included in this book. Without this learning, this book could not have been written.

Secondly, we thank those who have offered advice and information over the years and have contributed to our knowledge. Our specific thanks go to Jan Quallington for writing the Foreword to this edition, and all the other authors acknowledged through the text.

Our thanks go to Mike Reeves and Steve, Christopher and Victoria Orford for 'putting up with' our book writing, and the inconvenience this often causes.

Special acknowledgement goes to Barbara Carvalho, who celebrated 50 years as a nurse in September 2010; thank you, Mum, for your inspirational professional guidance and support.

We would like to dedicate this book to students past and present and hope that the *Fundamental Aspects of Legal, Ethical and Professional Issues in Nursing* (2nd Edition) will be a helpful tool for study and in nursing practice.

Sally Carvalho, Maggie Reeves and Jacquie Orford

Chronological table of statutes

Table of cases

Introduction

This book is aimed at those who are new to the fundamental concepts of legal, ethical and professional issues in nursing and who may want help in understanding them. This may be student nurses, when they come across these themes in their pre-registration nursing programme, or qualified nurses who are supervising such students in clinical practice. Hopefully, this book will provide a foundation.

It will look at the three issues – legal, professional and ethical – as separate entities. This is to help the reader understand the concepts in a better way. Although these topics will be looked at separately, in clinical nursing practice they are nearly always combined together. One way of imagining this is to consider a plait of hair. Each of the three strands is separate, but when plaited they are one.

When this occurs in the book, you will see this symbol:

For the purposes of this text, the term 'patient' will refer to service users as well as patients. The term 'nurse' relates to all fields of nursing and specialist community public health nurses.

Law and ethics are the frameworks within which professional issues are discussed and measured. This does not mean that the law has no morals or there is no law in professional aspects of nursing. They are intertwined.

The Health Service Circular 219.99 (Department of Health 1999) introduced the requirements for a revised nursing education programme. Under the Nursing and Midwifery Order 2001, the Nursing and Midwifery Council (NMC) is required to establish standards and minimum requirements for pre-registration nursing education. This book will help students to achieve the following NMC's (2010) generic competencies for entry to the register.

Competencies for entry to the NMC register

Domain 1: Professional values

All nurses must act first and foremost to care for and safeguard the public. They must practice autonomously and be responsible and accountable for safe, compassionate, person-centred, evidence-based nursing that respects and maintains dignity and human rights. They must show professionalism and integrity and work within recognised professional, ethical and legal frameworks. They must work in partnership with other health and social care professionals and agencies, service users, their carers and families, in all settings, including the community, ensuring that decisions about care are shared (Nursing and Midwifery Council 2010: 13).

Domain 2: Communication and interpersonal skills

All nurses must use excellent communication and interpersonal skills. Their communications must always be safe, effective, compassionate and respectful. They must communicate effectively using a wide range of strategies and interventions including the effective use of communication technologies. Where people have a disability, nurses must be able to work with service users and others to obtain the information needed to make reasonable adjustments that promote optimum health and enable equal access to services (Nursing and Midwifery Council 2010: 15).

Domain 3: Nursing practice and decision-making

All nurses must practice autonomously, compassionately, skilfully and safely, and must maintain dignity and promote health and well-being. They must assess and meet the full range of essential physical and mental health needs of people of all ages who come into their care. Where necessary they must be able to provide safe and effective immediate care to all people prior to accessing or referring to specialist services, irrespective of their field of practice. All nurses must also meet more complex and coexisting needs for people in their own nursing field of practice, in any setting, including hospital, community and at home. All practice should be informed by the best available evidence and comply with local and national guidelines. Decision-making must be shared with service users, carers and families and informed by critical analysis of a full range of possible interventions, including the use of up-to-date technology. All nurses must also understand how behaviour, culture, socioeconomic and other factors, in the care environment and its location, can affect health, illness, health outcomes and public health priorities, and take this into account in planning and delivering care (Nursing and Midwifery Council 2010: 17).

Domain 4: Leadership, management and team working

All nurses must be professionally accountable and use clinical governance processes to maintain and improve nursing practice and standards of healthcare. They must be able to respond autonomously and confidently to planned and uncertain situations, managing themselves and others effectively. They must create and maximise opportunities to improve services. They must also demonstrate the potential to develop further management and leadership skills during their period of preceptorship and beyond (Nursing and Midwifery Council 2010: 20).

The reader will be invited to cross reference the subjects in this book with all the learning outcomes of the Nursing and Midwifery Council Order (2010) and also The Code (Nursing and Midwifery Council 2008).

To get the most out of this book we suggest that you have a dedicated notebook/file and, if possible, access to a computer which you will use to undertake the recommended web-based activities to enhance your learning and reflection. These activities are marked with this symbol:✓🖐

This work can then be incorporated into your personal professional profile, which will help you to keep your knowledge and skills up to date throughout your nursing/midwifery career (Nursing and Midwifery Council 2008).

References

Department of Health (1999) *Health Service Circular HSC 1999/219 Making a Difference: Strengthening the nursing, midwifery and health visiting contribution to health and health care.* Department of Health, London

Nursing and Midwifery Council (2008) *The Code: Standards of conduct, performance and ethics for nurses and midwives.* Nursing and Midwifery Council, London

Nursing and Midwifery Council (2010) Standards for pre-registration nursing education. Nursing and Midwifery Council, London

Nursing and Midwifery Order 2001, SI 2002 No. 253

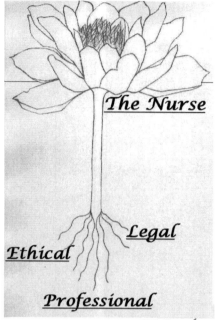

K.A. Ramsden

The public sees the nurse in full bloom, yet
nurses have their clinical practice firmly rooted
to the legal, ethical and professional foundations
of their education and training (SC)

Section I

This section introduces some important words and definitions.

- *Chapter 1* considers different aspects of the law.
- *Chapter 2* looks at how nurses behave and perform in practice.
- *Chapter 3* on ethics considers different issues related to conscience.

Although these topics are considered separately, in clinical nursing practice they are nearly always combined together like a plait of hair, as described in the Introduction. The law and ethics are the framework in which professional issues are discussed and measured.

CHAPTER I

What is law?

The aim of this chapter is to ensure that you have a basic understanding of the origin of the law and its relevance to your nursing practice. It covers aspects such as the main categories of law and how they are created. You will be given the opportunity to begin to identify some specific laws that influence nursing and healthcare.

The term liability is defined, and criminal and civil liability are briefly explained with some comparisons made between the two. Some offences that nurses could commit are identified. The court system is discussed so that you can gain an appreciation of the process in which you or a patient may become involved.

A broad understanding of the law is a requirement of many occupations and members of the public are becoming increasingly aware of their rights in law. Healthcare and nursing staff are no exception. The Code (Nursing and Midwifery Council 2008) states that registered nurses and midwives must act with integrity and adhere to the laws of the country in which they are practising.

Student nurses who are undertaking pre-registration education programmes also have to abide by the standards set by the Nursing and Midwifery Council; in addition to The Code, pre-registration student nurses must adhere to the recently published Guidance on Professional Conduct for nursing and midwifery students (Nursing and Midwifery Council 2010a) which applies to their supervised clinical practice and their academic studies. The current Standards for pre-registration nursing education (Nursing and Midwifery Council 2010b) state that student nurses must work within recognised professional, ethical and legal frameworks; students who fall below the expected standards will be held to account by the appropriate panel/committee within the Approved Education Institution (University) where they are studying towards their field-specific recordable qualification to ascertain their fitness to practice.

Where does law in the UK come from?

For simplicity, the focus here is on England and Wales which share the primary legislation of Westminster. There are many similarities with Scotland and Northern Ireland but there are also some differences and, as a result of legislation in 1998, Scotland and Northern Ireland can now make some laws relevant to their own country. This includes those relating to health issues (Elliott and Quinn, 2010).

There are two main origins of law, one made through Parliament (statutory law) and the other from case law (common law). There are others that are affected by laws laid down in Europe.

- Statutory law has been laid down and passed through Parliament and is often referred to as being 'on the statute book'. It is known as an Act of Parliament and is given a specific title and a date when it has completed the necessary stages.
- Common law has evolved over a considerable period of time and is based upon cases that have set a precedent. The judgments made are often referred to in subsequent cases and act as a 'yardstick' against which future decisions are made. One of the purposes of this is to try and ensure equity in decision-making. Common law can be traced back, in some instances, to 12th and 13th century England.

How is statutory law created through Parliament?

There are a series of stages that are followed in both the House of Commons and the House of Lords but they occur at different time intervals. A proposed piece of law may be first introduced in the House of Commons as a Bill. A Member of Parliament (MP), who is often a member of the Government of the time, introduces it. There are also Private Members' Bills. These are proposed by backbench MPs who have an interest in a particular subject which they believe should become law. An example is the Abortion Rights Bill presented by Nadine Dorries, MP in 2006 which failed to become law due to deep concerns expressed by the Government that did not support the bill. Private Member Bills may be first introduced in either the House of Lords or the House of Commons.

Usually a Green Paper is published and, if the topic is health related, this is distributed for consultation to interested parties, such as National Health Service trusts or health professional bodies. The Green Paper is often amended as a result of suggestions from a variety of sources, including pressure groups, or even an individual.

A White Paper follows. This sets out what the Government intends to do. The subsequent bill goes through a series of readings and stages (*Figure 1.1*), starting by giving it a title followed by an outline of the general principles (second reading). Voting takes place and a majority is needed for progression to the next stage. Once the general principles have been presented a committee is formed

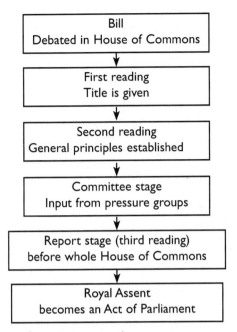

Figure 1.1. The process of creating statutory law.

which develops these in much more detail. The committee is important because it produces a detailed report for further consideration.

At the report stage, which is debated before the full House of Commons, amendments can be made. Voting occurs and if successful, the process of the three readings is repeated in the House of Lords.

Eventually, if both houses are in agreement with all the amendments, the Bill goes to the Monarch for Royal Assent, this signature transforming it to an Act of Parliament. However, the Act does not necessarily come into force (i.e. become law) when the Monarch signs it. Dates are either set in the Act itself or fixed by Statutory Instruments. Interestingly, some Acts have never been brought into force.

This process can be very slow, complex and time-consuming and a Bill may run out of time, never to become law. There are also various delaying tactics that can be employed.

Activity

Make a list of at least five Acts of Parliament that you think are relevant to nursing. Try to include the date that the Act was passed.

Box 1.1. Acts of Parliament
- Offences Against the Person Act 1861
- Suicide Act 1961
- Abortion Act 1967
- Misuse of Drugs Act 1971
- Health and Safety at Work Act 1974
- Mental Health Act 1983 (amended 2007)
- Public Health (Control of Diseases) Act 1984
- Children Act 1989 (amended 2004)
- Disability Discrimination Act 1995 (amended 2005)
- Data Protection Act 1998
- Public Interest Disclosure Act 1998
- Human Rights Act 1998
- Mental Capacity Act 2005
- National Health Service Act 2006
- Equity Act 2010

A vast number of Acts affect nursing and registered nurses and student nurses should be able to cite several by name and date. Check to see if your list contains any of those listed in *Box 1.1*. The ability to discuss the key aspects and relate them to practice will ensure that nurses do not break the law and will protect the interests of patients and patients.

Legal texts usually contain a table of statutes, if you want to check if there is an Act of Parliament about a particular issue. The important thing to remember is how these statutes affect your nursing practice.

Criminal and civil liability

Activity

Find a definition of liability.
You have probably come up with words such as legal obligation, being answerable for, responsible for ...

A crime is a public wrong that is considered unacceptable to society and thus the State prosecutes the offender providing there is sufficient evidence.

The opposite of a public wrong is a private wrong, whereby the offended individual (plaintiff or claimant) sues the wrongdoer in a civil action. The French word tort is often used in relation to these civil cases.

Older texts may refer to the word 'plaintiff' but Dimond (2008) stresses that the term 'claimant' should now be used.

Activity

Try to compare the two types of 'wrong' and make a table of the differences.

In *Table 1.1*, the term R *vs* Another refers to the way a criminal case is named. In this example the Crown Prosecution Service (CPS) takes the case to court. 'R' refers to Rex (King) or Regina (Queen). 'Another' is the surname of the other party involved, the accused. In civil cases the first name 'One' is that of the claimant while the second 'Other' is the defendant.

The seriousness of criminal and civil cases can vary. For example, a parking offence is a minor criminal offence compared to the extremely serious wrong of negligence. To confuse the issue, some incidents are both criminal offences and civil wrongs, e.g. assault.

Table 1.1. Criminal vs civil liability	
Criminal	*Civil*
Offence against the State	Civil wrong against the individual
May be intentional	Usually unintentional
Prosecuted by CPS: R *vs* Another	Sued One *vs* Other
Proof of guilt beyond all reasonable doubt	Liability on a balance of probabilities
Wide variety of sentences	
Prison, fine, community service, absolute discharge	Compensation, payment of damages, apology

In an ideal world, no nurse would ever commit a criminal offence or civil wrong but, unfortunately, some nurses do. The most serious offence would be murder. Murder is classed as a crime and is a common law offence; there is no such statute as a Murder Act.

Activity

Using the information given so far, identify some wrongs that a nurse could commit and classify each as either criminal or civil, and either bound by statutory or common law.

Dimond (2008: 12, 24) provides some examples of definitions of certain crimes, such as assault, battery, wounding and theft. She also lists some forms of civil action.

One of the most significant civil offences that may involve nurses is negligence, and this is discussed in *Chapter 6*.

Hierarchy of the courts

There are separate criminal and civil courts in England and most cities have a variety of each. Nearly all criminal cases start out in the Magistrates' Court, which

---

Activity

- Explore the website for the British and Irish Legal Information Institute (www.bailii.org). This website gives many examples of case law.
- To consolidate the information given about the hierarchy of the courts, you might find it helpful to access the structure of the current court system at www.hmcourts-service.gov.uk/aboutus/structure/index.htm

---

Associated study

- You may now want to find out a little more and, apart from the activities suggested so far, you could try to follow an Act of Parliament as it is created, making a few notes in your notebook. Valuable resources are newspapers, television and the Internet. Don't expect it to happen all at once though, remember the legislative process can be very slow!
- If you have ever been called for jury service reflect on what you learned in relation to the areas covered; or follow a case as it is reported in the press or on the Internet.
- Cases that have implications for nurses or healthcare are, of course, pertinent.

---

is presided over by lay individuals known as Justices of the Peace (JPs). If the accused pleads guilty to a minor offence, it can be dealt with there. Magistrates have a limited range of sentences they can impose. In other instances the magistrate will hold committal proceedings to decide if the case should go to the Crown Court.

The hierarchy of courts in England is as follows: County Courts and Crown Courts; Divisional Courts; High Courts; Courts of Appeal and the United Kingdom Supreme Court in England. Beyond this are the European Courts. In addition, there is the Coroner's Court that is empowered to investigate deaths which occur under specific circumstances. It functions differently from criminal and civil courts as its purpose is to find out the cause of death, not accuse anyone. Nurses may be required to attend a Coroner's Court as a witness to answer questions if they were involved in the deceased's care.

References

Dimond B (2008) *Legal aspects of nursing* (5th edn). Pearson Education, Harlow

Elliott C, Quinn F (2010) *English legal system* (11th edn). Longman, Harlow

Nursing and Midwifery Council (2008) *The Code: Standards of conduct, performance and ethics for nurses and midwives*. Nursing and Midwifery Council, London

Nursing and Midwifery Council (2010a) *Guidance on professional conduct for nursing and midwifery students* (2nd edn). Nursing and Midwifery Council, London

Nursing and Midwifery Council (2010b) *Standards for pre-registration nursing education*. Nursing and Midwifery Council, London

CHAPTER 2

Professional issues

This second chapter in *Section 1* focuses on introducing professional issues.

It starts by asking you to consider the terms professional, professionalisation and professionalism. The history and establishment of nursing's professional body, the Nursing and Midwifery Council (NMC), is discussed. You need to keep updated with the changes that are implemented by the NMC as part of your professional development. An outline of how nursing is controlled and its disciplinary procedures are included.

Professional issues are looked at as a separate subject and are then woven together with legal and ethical issues with examples from nursing practice.

What does professional mean?

Many books have been written discussing the idea of profession, professional, professionalism and professionalisation. What do they all mean?

Activity

Conduct a search to identify a definition for the following words:
Profession, professional, professionalism, professionalisation.

Burnard and Chapman (2005) indicate that a profession:

- Needs a body of specific knowledge based on research.
- Has knowledge that is passed on to new entrants to the profession and is guided by members of that profession.
- Places the needs of patients before the needs of the professional.
- Recognises that accountability for standards is judged by other professionals.

Fletcher and Buka (2007) state that a professional is a practitioner who has undergone a long course of training, the successful completion of which permits him or her to be entered on to a register maintained by the ruling body of that profession. The *Collins English Dictionary* (2003) describes professional as the way a professional behaves; the qualities or typical features of professionals, in other words professionalism. Tschudin (2006) suggests that the term professionalism is not only about what a group of people are, but also what they want to be.

Professionalisation means the process of attaining professional status. The consequence of this according to Rumbold (1999) is that nurses are no longer taught that they are, nor do they see themselves as, doctors' handmaids; they have become independent decision makers.

Activity

The current changes to pre-registration nurse education and training mean that nursing will be an all-graduate profession in the future (Nursing and Midwifery Council 2010). Consider whether or not this will push nursing closer to true professionalisation.

There are very many different ways of looking at this subject. Many of the books look at the history of nursing, the process of professionalisation and the quest for professionalism. However, most look at the nurse, midwife or specialist community public health nurse as a professional and how they are expected to behave in clinical practice.

The Nursing and Midwifery Council

The United Kingdom Central Council for Nursing, Midwifery and Health Visiting (UKCC) was established following the passing of the Nurses, Midwives and Health Visitors Act in 1979. There have since been amendments to the 1979 Act, notably in 1992 and 1997. It is interesting to note that the professional body here was concerned with the professions identified in its title while the legislation was named after the practitioners. The changes and developments since 1979 have necessitated legislative amendments. Under Section 60 of the Health Act (1999), the Nursing and Midwifery Council (NMC) was created and subsequently replaced the UKCC in 2002.

Activity

Search the NMC's website to find out how the members of the Council are appointed. www.nmc-uk.org

---

The NMC governing members are appointed in accordance with the Constitution of the NMC (Schedule 1 of the Nursing and Midwifery Order 2001). The main purpose of the NMC is to protect the public, which it does in a variety of ways, as detailed below.

Register of practitioners

The NMC maintains a register of practitioners and it controls who may or may not be listed on that register. The registration of nurses is not a recent occurrence; nurses were first listed as having been trained to a recognised standard in 1919. The body responsible for this was the General Nursing Council, which functioned up to 1979. There was a similar body which maintained a register of midwives.

Today's register is known as a live register because it lists those who are currently practising, not those who were once nurses and have ceased to practise. To be eligible for entry onto the register the nurse must have successfully completed a programme of education and training, and be of suitable character, usually verified by the university attended. The student will also need to pay the current fee set by the NMC for their initial entry onto the live register

Once on the live register there are requirements that have to be fulfilled by each nurse/midwife; renewal of registration is a requirement every three years, as is the payment of an annual fee, along with the completion of a Notification of Practice form. The NMC requires that practitioners sign to verify these requirements have been met and there is a mechanism for checking the accuracy of this. In addition, anyone can check via the NMC that an individual's registration is current. It is a criminal offence to claim to be a nurse when one has not qualified.

Although students are not on the register until they have successfully qualified, some of the requirements for renewal of registration form the basis of good practice. Students now have to keep a profile/portfolio of their learning and must still keep within the law.

Activity

In the previous three years:
- How many clinical hours must a nurse have worked?
- How many days study must have been completed?
- Which additional two areas have to be signed on the Notification of Practice form?

Education and training standards

The second function of the NMC is in relation to the education and training of nurses and midwives. Universities, National Health Service (NHS) trusts and other organisations, such as private nursing homes, HM prison services that provide nurse education, training, and/or practice experience, have set standards that students must meet. These are known, respectively, as the Standards for Education and the Standards for Competence, collectively known as the Standards for Pre-registration Nursing Education (NMC 2010). These standards ensure parity throughout the UK for any field of nursing the student is undertaking.

As health needs change so does the role of the nurse and the standards and requirements of course programmes reflect these.

The history of nursing clearly illustrates the many changes that have occurred since nurse training first began over a hundred years ago. It is a long time since nurses were apprentices learning 'on the job', following a medically-orientated model of training culminating in a State final examination. Nurses today undertake a programme of education, use evidence and research as a basis for their practice, and are accountable to their patients, their employer, themselves, the law and the profession.

Standards for conduct and practice

The NMC produces and regularly updates a variety of documents for all nurses. All registered nurses are a sent copy of the NMC Code (NMC 2008) when they qualify, and receive new versions when needed or on request. Universities often refer to the Code when teaching pre-registration students, and may require students to access it via the NMC website (www.nmc-uk.org). As the NMC website is accessible to the general public, anyone can obtain a copy of any publication. This is important as it facilitates the accountability of nursing to the public.

The professional body and practitioners regularly review these documents and feedback from the profession is an important contribution in raising standards of conduct and practice. The guidelines also form the basis upon which professional conduct is monitored.

Fitness to practice

The NMC considers and administers procedures related to fitness to practice. If a nurse or midwife is reported to the NMC, the following fitness to practice procedure will be followed:

- Allegation.
- Is there a case to answer?
  Yes: referral is made to the appropriate committee
  No: case closed
- Adjudication (the appropriate committee makes its decision).
- Outcomes and actions: the register is amended to reflect the committee's decision
- Appeals and restorations: 28 days are allowed to lodge an appeal against the committee's decision

Activity

- You might like to familiarise yourself with the three current NMC fitness to practice committees:
- Investigation Committee
- Conduct and Competence Committee
- Health Committee

The NMC in its role to protect the public considers all complaints made to them.

After 5 years, a nurse or midwife, who has been struck off can apply to be reinstated on the live register. However, the NMC reserves the right not to reinstate them.

The above complaints procedure is set in motion once a written, signed complaint is received by the NMC stating who did what, to whom and when. Anyone can make a complaint: patients, their relatives, visitors, colleagues from another discipline, student nurses, managers or employers.

The complaint is investigated by the NMC in which evidence, statements and witnesses are gathered. This is a formalised professional procedure and the purpose is to obtain information to prove beyond reasonable doubt that there is a case to answer. The case has to be one that is serious enough to justify removing the practitioner's name from the register. Interim suspension of the nurse may occur if the offence is very serious. Do not forget the main purpose is to protect the public, not to punish practitioners.

All complaints go to the respective NMC panels. The members are external applicants except for the chair who is an elected member of the NMC and one lay person (non-nursing) who has applied via the NMC public advertisement. Following investigation of complaints the following may occur:

- The case may be closed.
- The complaint may be referred to the Conduct and Competence Committee for a further formal hearing.
- The complaint may be referred to the Health Committee.
- A formal caution as to future conduct, which is monitored, may be issued.

If the complaint is forwarded for further consideration it is heard in public to reflect the NMC's public accountability. The format of the hearing is similar to a criminal court. The aim is to determine whether the facts are proven and if this is the case, if it is serious professional misconduct. The NMC has the power to take a variety of actions depending on the outcome of the hearing.

Activity
- Access the NMC website: www.nmc-uk.org and identify what the NMC actions following a hearing for professional misconduct might be.
- Find out how the Health Committee may be involved, how they hear a case and the options open to them.

Your examples will clearly demonstrate the profession's determination to protect the public.

This brings the discussion round to the NMC Code and the other supporting texts regarding medicines/records/specialist documents for age/client groups published by the NMC to guide and advise nurses who must behave in an appropriate way.

The legal-ethical-professional link

When the NMC Code was written, it was constructed within the laws of England, Wales, Scotland and Northern Ireland. It was based on *ethical* principles and is a *professional* document that adheres to the *law*. A working knowledge of the Code is expected of all nurses by the NMC.

Activity

To summarise answer the following questions. Most of the answers can be found in this text, through your own knowledge or by using the Internet.

* If the NMC Code is a guide or a standard, what purpose does it serve?
* Who is it designed for?
* Who wrote it?
* Name the law that established the body that wrote it.
* What types of issues does it cover?
* What powers does it have?
* What consequences could arise from putting the Code into practice or ignoring its content.

References

Burnard P, Chapman CM (2005) *Professional and ethical issues in nursing: The Code of professional conduct* (3rd edn). Baillière Tindall, London

Fletcher L, Buka P (2007) *A legal framework for caring* (3rd edn). Macmillan, Basingstoke

Nursing and Midwifery Council (2008) *The Code: Standards of conduct, performance and ethics for nurses and midwives*. Nursing and Midwifery Council, London

Nursing and Midwifery Council (2010) *Standards for pre-registration nursing education*. Nursing and Midwifery Council, London

Rumbold G (1999) *Ethics in nursing practice* (3rd edn). Baillière Tindall, London

Tschudin V (2006) *Ethics in nursing: The caring relationship* (3rd edn). Elsevier, Edinburgh

CHAPTER 3

Values, morals and ethics

Ethics is a subject used every day. You may not identify your decisions as using 'ethics' but, whatever you do in life, there are reasons why you follow certain paths. Over the centuries people have looked at why individuals follow different paths and have considered frameworks to identify trends. This is loosely what ethical theory is.

Thompson et al (2006) define ethics (which is from the Greek word '*ethos*' – the spirit of a community) as the collective belief-and-value system of any moral community, or social or professional group. It is one of the ways by which a group/community can live in harmony. This definition introduces two more words: 'morals' and 'values'. Again according to Thompson et al (2006), morals and morality refer to the domain of personal values and the rules of behaviour regulating social interactions.

Morality and ethics deal with human relationships – how humans treat other beings so as to promote mutual welfare, growth, creativity and meaning as they strive for good over bad and right over wrong (Thiroux and Krasemann 2007).

Values are personal and are, according to Simon (1973),

One of a set of personal beliefs and attitudes about the truth, beauty and worth of any thought, object or behaviour. Values are action oriented and give direction and meaning to one's life.

Values are the starting points for morality and ethics.

These three concepts of values, morals and ethics can be seen to interact and relate to each other. Each person's morals and ethics develop over a lifetime and originate from a variety of things valued. Thus, these values and morals have been acquired from a variety of sources, which will be looked at in this chapter.

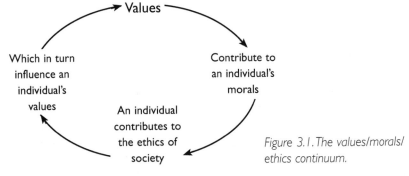

Figure 3.1. The values/morals/ethics continuum.

These concepts and definitions will now be pulled together to make more sense of them.

What is a value?

> **Activity**
> Try to think of a definition of a value, and then consider what you value and why.

It is not easy to define exactly what constitutes a value. Perhaps your definition of a value indicated that it is something that is very important to you, it is personal, precious and, very often, is something that you would take risks to defend. Burnard and Chapman (2005) suggest that to find out what a person values and why it is valued, it would be useful to look at anthropology, geography, sociology, psychology and theology, as they relate to that individual. How do all these 'ologies' help you decide who or what has influenced what you value?

> **Activity**
> Consider all the 'ologies' listed above and relate them to your personal circumstances.

- Looking at *anthropology* could identify your cultural background and your social situation

    Where were you brought up? What was expected of you as a child in different circumstances? What sort of family you were raised in? Apart from your family, who else had influence over you in your childhood?

- *Geography* may identify the environment that you were brought up in and exposed to.

    What are your attitudes towards conservation, smoking, urban areas, animals, rural areas, beggars, water and sunlight?

- *Sociology* may help you analyse 'why' you value certain things and the influence those around you had or still have on you.

    Who has influenced you the most throughout your life – particular individuals or groups of people? Do you still value the things that these individuals or groups value? If you no longer value these things, why?

- *Psychology* on the other hand may indicate what sort of person you are and why you respond to external influences as you do.

  Are you easily persuaded to change your mind? Are you aware of how you tend to respond to different circumstances? Do you find advertising easily or rarely influences you?

- *Theology* may also be a great influence on your value system and be tied up with the other issues considered above. Your spiritual or religious point of view may be the most significant factor of all.

  When you make a decision does your religious (or other) belief system influence what you do? Do you find you value things that others seem to consider unimportant? Are you conscious of 'trying to do the right thing'? Are your beliefs about 'right' and 'wrong' different from some of your colleagues?

Taking all your answers to the above questions, you may have begun to start thinking about what you actually value and where you first got that notion.

Tschudin (2006) and Cuthbert and Quallington (2008) argue that values are not static, they help us to navigate our lives on a personal and professional level, they can also be the means and instruments for making decisions, be ends in themselves and define us as people. Values can be seen as dynamic in that they change and develop throughout life. Not all values are held to be as important as others; there is a tendency to put them into hierarchies.

Activity

Here are some other things to consider:
- Decide what it is you actually value – make a list.
- Taking your list put your most important value at the top then prioritise the rest.
- Look back several years and ask yourself if each item on your list was a value then and whether it was as important to you.

A hierarchy of values is where one value is at the top of your priorities and others are of lesser importance. There will be some things on your list that you will never change. They are fundamentally 'you'. Within the NMC Code (NMC 2008), the standard 'Treat people as individuals', states that you must not discriminate in any way against those in your care. Nurses practise in diverse cultural environments and must take care not to offend patients' values and beliefs.

One value that you may never change is that of conscientious objection. Current legislation does permit the nurse or midwife to conscientiously object to providing treatment for patients under Article 4(2) of the Abortion Act 1967 England, Scotland, Wales, and under Article 38(2) of the Human Fertilisation and Embryology Act 1990. If a nurse were to conscientiously object to providing treatment for a patient under the aforementioned legislation, the NMC (2008) states:

> *The individual must inform someone in authority if they experience problems that prevent the individual from working within the code or other nationally agreed standards.*

The *Janaway v Salford* case clearly defines what constitutes 'treatment' in relation to 'conscientious objection'. This concept relates to issues contrary to your moral beliefs or a strongly held value, such as the sanctity of life, on which you are never prepared to compromise. However, other things will be more flexible and adaptable. For example, do you value your health? Very few people would say 'no' to that question. How do you value your health? could be a more searching question. The following are some of the answers that student nurses have given:

- By not smoking.
- By keeping fit.
- By eating a healthy diet.
- By practising safe sex.
- By trying to keep stress free.

Look at one of these answers to see how it could be adapted. Many people aim to eat a healthy diet. Those who truly eat a healthy diet may on occasions eat very unhealthily. This does not mean that they do not value a healthy diet, rather that the individual can be flexible about this particular value.

Another value, such as the sanctity of life, may be more difficult to compromise. This could be an individual's bedrock value that will never change whatever the circumstances.

One of the important things about looking at values is that you clarify for yourself what concepts you value. This clarification can help you understand why another nurse or a patient irritates you. A nursing colleague, for example, may value the concept of 'work' in a different way; a patient may irritate because his or her manners are culturally different from yours. Conversely, your friends may all have the same approach to the balance of academic work and social life. People often make friends with those who share similar values.

As Uustal (1978) warned,

> *If you do not take time to examine and articulate your values, you will not be fully effective with patients.*

This could also relate to your personal relationships.

What you value influences your moral behaviour and the decisions that you make in life. Your values can also be the framework on which you judge others. It is important to remember this when considering the often repeated phrase that nurses must be non-judgemental. Perhaps it is wise to acknowledge that we do judge others but remember that this judgement must not affect the way we nurse. It is what we do with our judgements rather than having them in the first place that matters; how a nurse behaves in a professional manner.

Refer back to *Figure 3.1* and see that although you may have many and varied values, they all contribute to your personal set of morals. Each person has a different set depending on all the 'ologies' referred to earlier. Your life experiences may also have affected how you react to your past values and those of others. Individually, however, our consciences are sensitive to these values. These values may make you aware of factors that prick your conscience and help you decide the appropriate path.

Activity

Because people are all different, the things that affect your conscience may be different from what affects your friend's conscience. Consider:

- What affects your conscience?
- What helps you decide what is right or wrong?
- What feelings do you experience/what reactions do you receive if you do right or wrong?
- What do you do if someone else takes a different approach from you?

The answers you have given to the questions posed in the box will be very personal, but there will be sentiments that are common to all. Statements like 'feeling guilty', 'feeling uncomfortable with myself', 'angry with myself' and 'worried about what others think' have all been expressed by students in the past.

23

Equally, there are reactions when something felt to be 'right' has been done, feelings of smugness, relief or regret. Other people may not appreciate you 'doing the right thing' because it in turn makes them feel guilty. Their reaction may be one of hostility, rejection or hurt. Such reactions could lead to a confrontation or being ignored. Acceptance of another's viewpoint is not straightforward. If you value something, you will defend it and so will the other person!

Relating values and morals to nursing practice

In nursing, as in life in general, you are presented with all sorts of situations to which you will react. Problems come to you that have to be dealt with. The way you deal with each problem will be based on the values that you have and the moral standpoint that you take.

Many of the problems you face have to do with things like honesty, doing good, having a choice, valuing someone's worth and being fair about something.

Philosophers have tried to put these issues into a coherent order. Thiroux and Krasemann (2007) are two such philosophers who have made a simple list of ideas into which values could slot. This list/framework or set of principles provides a way of looking at such issues. They could be quite minor in character or be very weighty issues.

The list consists of the following:

- *The value of life*: Individuals should revere life and accept death.
- *Goodness or rightness*: Individuals should promote goodness over badness (sometimes called beneficence), cause no harm or badness (sometimes called non-maleficence), and prevent badness or harm.
- *Justice or fairness*: This refers to equality of distribution.
- *Honesty or truth-telling*: This includes providing meaningful communication.
- *Individual freedom or autonomy*: This includes the freedom of individuals to choose their own ways and means of being moral, within the framework of the above four principles.

When providing healthcare for patients, pre-registration students in particular, often experience a challenge to their own values when faced with situations that are new and that require them to make decisions that oppose their own beliefs. The NMC (2008) states that the nursing and midwifery professions must provide anti-discriminatory healthcare, thus issues such as responsibility, accountability, and negligence need to be explored in relation to personal and professional values.

Activity

Access the *Values Exchange* developed with Seedhouse (2009) (www.values-exchange.com). This is a decision support programme that will help you to explore your ethical beliefs in relation to a range of scenarios. Access one of the cases and work through it.

Scenarios

Consider each of the following principles and scenarios. Work on each scenario and the accompanying questions. You can work on your own or discuss the issues raised with friends.

The value of life

In February 2010, a registered nurse was struck off the register by the NMC. The nurse was found guilty of a number of charges, most notably the neglect of a dying patient. The nurse failed to provide the most basic of nursing care; the patient was left soaking in urine and did not receive pressure area care or change in position for comfort.

- Discuss the value of life principle in this situation.
- Consider any literature you may find.
- Discuss what alternative courses of action the practitioner could have taken to prevent a similar situation.
- Which part of the NMC Code is relevant to this scenario?

Goodness or rightness

A visitor to the ward states that she is the new nurse specialist attached to the ward (she has no identification badge). She wants to see a patient's notes prior to sorting out discharge requirements with the patient.

- Discuss the principle of goodness or rightness in this situation.
- Consider any literature you may find.
- Debate alternative strategies you might employ if you were approached by the visitor and the consequences of each.
- Which part of the NMC Code is relevant in this scenario?

Justice or fairness

Nurses can often be very short of time. Your ward is very busy and one of your student colleagues is admitted to your ward. You spend quite a long time talking to her. Another patient, who is known by the nursing team for enjoying long conversations because she is normally quite socially isolated, says that she is really lonely and asks you to listen to something that she wants to tell you. You say you are sorry, but you are too busy.

- Discuss the principle of justice or fairness in this situation.
- Consider any literature you may find – do not forget other NMC publications.
- Debate your reasons for giving preference to one patient and the consequences of this.
- Which part of the NMC Code is relevant in this situation?

Truth-telling or honesty

A male patient who is married with a young child is diagnosed as HIV positive. You know from discussions with him that he has other sexual partners. His wife asks you what is wrong with her husband.

- Discuss the principle of truth-telling or honesty in this situation.
- Consider any literature you may find.
- Debate alternative strategies you might employ if asked this question and the consequences of each.
- Which part of the NMC Code is relevant in this situation?

Individual freedom or autonomy

For several days, a 17-year-old patient has refused to eat and drink. When you ask her why, she says it is because of her religious principles.

- Discuss the principle of individual freedom or autonomy in this situation.
- Consider any literature you may find.
- Debate the different reactions from the people involved in the life of this teenager, and the potential consequences of her decision.
- Which part of the NMC Code is relevant in this situation?

You will notice from the questions asked following each scenario that the NMC Code has been referred to on each occasion. This was a deliberate ploy because it is important to be able use the Code in specific circumstances.

The legal-ethical-professional link

The questions illustrate the 'plait' referred to in the Introduction. Although legal, ethical and professional issues are separate, in nursing practice they are normally entwined.

References

Burnard P, Chapman CM (2005) *Professional and ethical issues in nursing: The Code of professional conduct* (3rd edn). Baillière Tindall, London

Cuthbert S, Quallington J (2008) *Values for care practice*. Reflect Press Ltd, Exeter

Janaway v Salford HA [1988] 3 WLR 1350(HL)

Nursing and Midwifery Council (2008) *The Code: Standards of conduct, performance and ethics for nurses and midwives*. Nursing and Midwifery Council, London

Seedhouse D (2009) *Ethics: The heart of health care* (3rd edn). Wiley-Blackwell, Chichester

Simon SB (1973) Meeting yourself halfway. Cited in: Tschudin V (1992) *Values: A primer for nurses*. Baillière Tindall, London

Thiroux JP, Krasemann KW (2007) *Ethics: Theory and practice* (9th edn). Prentice Hall, New Jersey

Thompson IE, Melia KM, Boyd KM (2006) *Nursing ethics* (5th edn). Churchill Livingstone, Edinburgh

Tschudin V (2006) *Ethics in nursing: The caring relationship* (3rd edn). Elsevier Ltd, Edinburgh

Uustal D (1978) Values clarification in nursing: Application to practice. *American Journal of Nursing* **Dec**: 2053–63

Section 2

In this section you will begin to see how the three strands, legal, ethical and professional introduced in *Section 1*, are plaited together and applied to your practice. The topic areas covered in this section are:

- Responsibility
- Accountability
- Negligence

CHAPTER 4

Responsibility

Some definitions will be looked at first and then you will be asked to identify aspects of your everyday life for which you are responsible. As soon as you start your education and training as a nurse, you begin to be responsible for a variety of things and when you go out into clinical practice, even for the first time, this list grows. Discussion of some of these will help you to understand the implications of accepting responsibility.

As a registered nurse, you are responsible for students you teach and supervise. If you are a clinical mentor and/or assessor for a student your role encompasses more than just responsibility, you are accountable for that student, as will be discussed later in this section.

Activity
- Write a definition for the word 'responsibility'.
- What does responsibility mean to you?

Compare your answers to a selection of definitions provided by other nursing students:

- Liable, dependable.
- An obligation, duty.
- Being trusted.
- Completion of tasks.
- Willingness to do something.
- Something given to you when you've shown you can do it/learned it.
- Being in charge of a given situation.
- Taking charge of expectations.
- Standing by what you believe in.
- Being aware/concerned for others.

Some students used phrases like 'being accountable for your actions','making intelligent, educated judgements', and 'facing the consequences'. You will see as you progress through *Section 2* that these phrases are more akin to a definition of accountability, so if you wrote similar definitions keep them for later as there is a link between responsibility and accountability.

Cuthbert and Quallington (2008) identify that responsibility relates to accepting a task or duty that you have been given. Thus, there are two components to responsibility: one being asked or charged to do something and the other accepting this task willingly.

Activity
Make a list of things you are responsible for in your everyday life.

It is impossible to give a definitive list as we are all individuals, but your list may contain items such as caring for children, exercising the dog, feeding the cat, taxing and insuring the car, doing the shopping and laundry, and paying household bills.

Activity
Select one task from your list and identify what this responsibility involves and why.

There may be some very sound reasons for undertaking a responsibility. The list below provides some of these.

- The law says you must.
- Fear of punishment.
- It is the right thing to do – morally/ethically/honestly.
- It is what is expected by others or society in general.
- It may be because you always have done it and are conditioned into doing it without thinking any further.

Responsibility is personal and derives from being a citizen and human being. As a nurse, if you have agreed to undertake a task there is an expectation that you will do it to the best of your ability, safely and correctly. Safety is the required level of ability for students in the early part of the pre-registration course. This requires you to have:

- *Knowledge* of what the task is and why you are doing it.
- The *skill* to perform the task.
- An appropriate *attitude* to the patient.

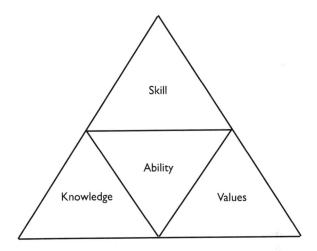

Figure 4.1. Pre-requisites for responsibility.

This is likely to include the ability to communicate effectively and demonstrate that you value the patient's individuality, dignity and privacy.

The triangle in *Figure 4.1* illustrates the link between these prerequisites. According to Bergman (1981), ability is one of the preconditions necessary to become firstly responsible and ultimately accountable. You will return to Bergman's work later in this section.

Student nurses' responsibilities

From the first day of any pre-registration course, students take on responsibilities. Attitudes to one's own learning and that of other students are very important. The student is immediately responsible for attending lectures, punctuality, respecting others' desire and need to learn, being committed to and involved in the course, and being self-directed and motivated. Other areas of responsibility require you to act upon advice, guidance and feedback from academic staff and begin to develop your portfolio of learning. These may seem very obvious and are not exclusive to nursing students.

Student nurses are also responsible for their health and are required to have the relevant immunisations and vaccinations prior to commencing clinical practice. Another important area includes the need for a criminal record bureau check (CRB) to ensure that the student is a suitable person to be caring for others and the student has a responsibility to provide any relevant information relating to this. There are links here again with professional issues because, as you discovered earlier, the Nursing and Midwifery Council must ensure that the public is protected, hence there are mandatory sessions that students will have to attend at their university, such as manual handling training.

The list below identifies general areas of responsibility that the student nurse has in relation to the NMC (2010) guidance on professional conduct for nursing and midwifery students:

- Treat people as individuals.
- Respect a person's confidentiality.
- Collaborate with those in your care.
- Ensure you gain consent.
- Maintain clear professional boundaries.
- Work as part of a team.
- Recognise and work within your limits of competence.
- Ensure your skills and knowledge are up to date.
- Be open and honest.
- Act with integrity.
- Protect people from harm.
- Uphold the reputation of the nursing and midwifery professions.

Activity

In addition to the above responsibilities, what do you think student nurses will be responsible for on their first clinical placement?

It can be seen that nurses have responsibilities to patients, relatives, colleagues, society and themselves; however, these responsibilities should reflect the level of education and training of the nurse or student (NMC 2008, 2010).

Responsibility is often linked to roles: different roles have different responsibilities. Compare the responsibilities of students on their first placement with more senior students, or students with registered nurses. Adult field nurses may have different roles from child, mental health or learning disabilities nurses. If you are a clinical mentor, your role will be expanded to encompass this with additional responsibilities.

Activity

- The NMC's (2010) guidance on professional conduct for nursing and midwifery students provides a more comprehensive list of pre-registration student responsibilities.
- Access the current guidelines to familiarise yourself with them.

Implications of responsibility

If you refer back to some of the reasons why you undertake the personal responsibilities you listed at the start of this section, the implications of failing to take them show similarities. For example, as a nurse, if your practice contravenes the Health and Safety at Work Act (1974) there may be legal implications for you and/or your employer. If you fail to practise to the standard set by any of the NMC guidelines, a complaint may be made. In the first instance, as a student, this may be to your clinical mentor or clinical manager who may address you and advise you how to improve your practice. Continuing failure to practice appropriately could result in failure to achieve the learning outcomes required by the NMC. This could mean that a student would be unable to continue training.

If there is serious inappropriate behaviour, such as theft or patient abuse, immediate withdrawal from the nurse education and training course is likely, in addition to possible legal consequences.

Registered nurses who fail to practice or behave professionally may be disciplined by the NMC, as described in *Section 1*.

Most nurses, at some time during their careers, experience occasions when their conscience is troubled by aspects of their work or that of others. This can result in feelings of discomfort, anxiety and concern about continuing as a nurse. For students with little experience this can be quite distressing and should be voiced so that they can be supported through such experiences and learn from them. Support is available from clinical mentors, managers, clinical link/liaison teachers, personal tutors and other academic staff as well as other students and nursing colleagues.

Even when qualified, nurses will often find such support is required. These are ethical issues so, once again, the three strands which form the basis of this text are woven together.

It can be seen that student nurses become responsible very early on and need to understand what this means and entails. The NMC's (2010) guidance on professional conduct for nursing and midwifery students emphasises this important aspect both to protect the public and enhance the profession of nursing.

References

Bergman R (1981) Accountability: Definition and dimension. *International Nursing Review* **28**(2): 53–9

Cuthbert S, Quallington J (2008) *Values for care practice*. Reflect Press Ltd, Exeter

Nursing and Midwifery Council (2008) *The Code: Standards of conduct, performance and ethics for nurses and midwives*. Nursing and Midwifery Council, London

Nursing and Midwifery Council (2010) *Guidance on professional conduct for nursing and midwifery students* (2nd edn). Nursing and Midwifery Council, London

CHAPTER 5

Accountability

By the end of this chapter you should be able to define accountability and give examples of the origins of accountability with reference to a variety of literature. You should be able to differentiate it from responsibility and identify the prerequisites of accountability. To whom you are accountable will be determined and some aspects of accountability in practice will be discussed. The consequences of accountability in relation to standards of care will be outlined. The NMC Code (NMC 2008) clearly establishes that registered nurses and midwives are accountable for their practice, thus accountability is an integral part of professional practice. What does this mean?

Some of the phrases given by students in *Chapter 4* for responsibility were actually more indicative of accountability. Examples included: making judgements, being called to account and justifying what you did, being answerable for and facing the consequences of one's actions.

Many people confuse responsibility and accountability, perhaps because there are links between them. Responsibility and accountability are closely connected but are not the same, thus they should not to be used synonymously. Savage and Moore's (2004) study identified that accountability required further definition among the study's participants.

Bergman (1981) illustrates the links in her model of the preconditions leading to accountability (see *Figure 5.1*).

Figure 5.1. Preconditions leading to accountability.

You will remember that the lower levels of this triangle were used when discussing responsibility earlier.

Authority arises from the position you are given and accept, which in turn allows you the power to make decisions. Decision-making involves making judgements in a wide variety of circumstances. This suggests that you also need to be autonomous, being given the freedom to make those choices. Walsh (2002) includes this in saying that to be accountable is to have responsibility both to self and others while having the authority to act autonomously. Lewis and Batey (1982) suggest that authority is needed to carry out actions for which you can be held accountable whilst Pattison (2009) links the degree of accountability to the degree of authority.

Where does the authority come from?

As a student in the early stages of a nursing programme, authority is given to you by the education and training body, in partnership with the university where you are studying. When you undertake clinical practice it is your clinical mentor who gives you the authority to participate in care delivery. At first this is under supervision but, as you gain experience, authority increases in line with your more senior status. Both responsibility and authority are linked to this developing role where you may be judged as capable of giving some aspects of care unaided. Once qualified the authority is given by the NMC, as part of being on the register, and by your employer within the job description which applies to your post. You are now considered to be accountable.

Professionally, you may delegate responsibility to someone else but not accountability; this remains with the person doing the delegation who must ensure that whoever they ask to undertake a task/duty is able to perform that task/duty correctly. Individuals asked to perform the task/duty must say if they do not feel capable in accordance with the NMC Code (2008). This forms an important part of the relationship between a student nurse and clinical mentor.

Student nurses are never professionally accountable in the same way as registered nurses and the NMC (2008) states that it is the registered nurse with whom you are working who is professionally accountable for the consequences of your actions and omissions during the delegation of tasks/duties. However, as a student you can be called to account by the law or the university who is educating and training you.

To summarise, professional responsibility and accountability are not the same. The key differences are:

- Responsibility has to be accepted.
- You can be inexperienced but still have responsibilities, whereas accountability comes with experience.
- Responsibility can be delegated but accountability cannot.
- Someone must give you authority before you can be accountable.
- Accountability requires you to make autonomous decisions.
- You must be prepared to answer for your actions to be accountable.

Activity

List who you think the registered nurse is accountable to.

Figure 5.2 illustrates how the law is an integral part of nurses' accountability.

Student nurses who undertake any aspect of care which the mentor is unaware of ('going off on a frolic of their own!') will have put themselves into a position of being accountable. The student could be accountable to all the individuals in *Figure 5.2* except the NMC. Can you recall from *Section 1* why this is an exception?

Figure 5.2. Spider diagram of nurses' accountability. Adapted from Dimond (2002: 5).

Student nurses' duties can include what they say, write or do. In the case of what they say, they are accountable because no one else puts words in their mouth. What they write requires countersigning by a registered practitioner so, although they are responsible, the registered nurse is accountable. *Chapter 8* will explore the standards required in relation to written communication.

The same situation arises in relation to what you do, as it should be under supervision or with the knowledge of the mentor who considers you to be competent. This would be in agreement with your own perception since the NMC (2010) indicates that you must seek help from a competent practitioner until you have acquired the requisite knowledge, ability and skill.

Two expressions are used in relation to accountability – acts of commission and acts of omission. If you provide care that you know is of a poor or incorrect standard, for example, dragging a patient up the bed, this is an act of commission for which you could be held accountable. Although you may have repositioned the patient and made him or her more comfortable the manner in which you did it was unacceptable. You should also consider things not done which should have been done. These are called acts of omission.

Both qualified nurses and students can commit acts of commission and acts of omission.

Activity

Can you think of three acts of omission?

Answer

- You may have thought of not completing some type of chart, such as an observation or fluid balance chart although you did perform the task.
- Failing to follow a procedure or policy correctly, e.g., not informing a detained mental health patient of his or her rights under the Mental Health Act (1983).
- Not passing on information to the rest of the multidisciplinary team despite the patient giving you permission.
- Not explaining a child's care to a parent.

Acts of omission are often not intentional. However, the consequences for the patient could be serious as you will see later in *Chapter 6* on negligence, as the student is accountable under common law. Nurses are expected to uphold the good standing and reputation of the profession, irrespective of their status.

Professional accountability incorporates legal, moral and ethical aspects and sets a very high standard for nurses.

Activity

Identify the variety of sanctions that could be imposed by the following and explain why

• NMC   • Colleague   • Society   • Employer   • Self

The implications of accountability may appear to be similar to those identified at the end of the chapter on responsibility.

The severity of the sanction depends on what you have done but anything that means you cannot continue as a nurse can be catastrophic. Being removed from the register as a result of a criminal conviction or being found guilty of professional misconduct may end the career of a registered nurse. Being dismissed from the course as a student will prevent you from getting on the register in the first place. Sometimes an employer may dismiss you but you may still be able to work elsewhere as a nurse provided that you remain on the professional register. The views of colleagues or your own feelings of disgust or self-hatred can be very hard to deal with and may result in your choosing to leave nursing. Moral and ethical implications can be just as strong as legal or professional sanctions, the latter are simply imposed by someone else.

To help you apply all this to practice try the following activity.

Activity

• Read the following fictional scenarios and decide who you think is responsible and/or accountable.
• Use Bergman's prerequisites of accountability mentioned earlier and think about whether the student should be able to undertake the duty.

Scenario 1

Mary wishes to have a shower and as you helped her to have a bath two days ago you feel confident that you are able to do this unsupervised. Mary finishes her shower and asks you to pass her the towel. Unfortunately she drops it on the shower floor where it rapidly becomes too wet to use. 'Don't worry, Mary', you say, 'I'll just pop and get another one, I won't be a minute'. On your return you find Mary unconscious on the floor, half out of the shower. She appears to have tried to step out of the shower to put on her dressing gown.

Scenario 2

You have a very good clinical mentor who has worked with you all morning. Together you have just finished washing an elderly, mentally ill and dependent gentleman. This is a new experience as most of the patients you have met have been self-caring. The gentleman is now comfortably sitting in a chair so your mentor says, 'Just comb his hair and do his mouth and I'll start the drug round, join me when you've finished.' She disappears before you have time to reply. You are aware that this patient has a history of swallowing difficulties and is an epileptic.

Conclusion

However accountability is defined, it is important to remember that the courts are the final venue for the resolution of disputes in medicine and nursing (Pattison 2009).

References

Bergman R (1981) Accountability: Definition and dimension. *International Nursing Review* **28**(2): 53–9

Dimond B (2002) *Legal aspects of nursing* (3rd edn). Longman, Harlow

Lewis F, Batey M (1982) Clarifying autonomy and accountability in nursing services. Cited in: Jones M (1996) *Accountability in practice*. Quay Books, Mark Allen Publishing, Salisbury

Nursing and Midwifery Council (2008) *The Code: Standards of conduct, performance and ethics for nurses and midwives*. Nursing and Midwifery Council, London

Nursing and Midwifery Council (2010) *Guidance on professional conduct for nursing and midwifery students* (2nd edn). Nursing and Midwifery Council, London

Pattison D (2009) *Medical law and ethics* (2nd edn). Sweet and Maxwell, London

Savage J, Moore L (2004) *Interpreting accountability: An ethnographic study of practice nurses, accountability and multidisciplinary team decision-making in the context of clinical governance*. Royal College of Nursing, London

Walsh M (ed) (2002) *Watson's clinical nursing and related sciences* (6th edn). Baillière Tindall, London

CHAPTER 6

Negligence

The first two chapters in this section have focused on professional issues in relation to nursing practice but this final chapter looks at one legal implication of poor practice to complete the picture, that of negligence. Dimond (2008) identifies that nurses who do not meet the accepted standards of practice or who perform or carry out their duties carelessly potentially run the risk of being negligent.

Activity
- Find a legal definition for the word 'negligence'.
- Search for the case *Anderson B in Blyth v Birmingham Waterworks Co* [1856] 11EXCH 781. This case explores issues related to 'negligence'.

Activity
Can you recall what type of 'wrong' negligence is?

In this chapter we will look at some actual cases (which have been simplified for this book) to determine the components that have to be proved by the claimant if he or she is to win the case. Reference is made to professional documents that help to set standards of care and that may be used in legal situations.

Activity
To whom does the term 'claimant' refer?

The defendant is either the individual practitioner who is alleged to have caused the harm or the organisation which employs that practitioner. Check back to *Chapter 1* if you have forgotten how this is referred to in most literature. In most cases which involve nurses it is the employer who is taken to court as the purpose of negligence is to sue for compensation and very few nurses would be able to pay if the case is proven. However, the NMC (2008) does advise nurses to have some form of indemnity insurance. In 2009/10, 6652 claims of clinical negligence were recorded by the NHS Litigation Authority which resulted in compensation payments totalling £787 million. The NHS Redress Act 2006 (England and Wales) sought to provide recipients of NHS care the opportunity to seek redress without having to commence court proceedings.

Activity

Access the NHS Litigation Authority at www.nhsla.com and compare the number of clinical negligence claims and payments made for 2009/10 and 2008/09.

Activity

Access the NHS Redress Act 2006 at www.legislation.gov.uk and identify which claims can be addressed under this legislation.

The reason the employer is identified in negligence cases is because employers take responsibility for the actions of the employee. This is known as the principle of vicarious liability and the employer must be insured against employees' actions which may cause harm to colleagues and/or patients. Vicarious liability only applies if the employee is working within his or her normal employment which is explained in the contract of employment and job description (Fletcher and Buka 2007). The basis of proof is one of a balance of probabilities, which means that there must be a greater than 50% chance of the act causing or contributing to harm (Moody 2001) and that there was a failure to follow a reasonable standard of care.

Harm is one of the four aspects which claimants must prove. These aspects or components of negligence are illustrated in *Figure 6.1*.

Duty of care

One of the main roles of a nurse is to care for patients and it is not usually difficult for the claimant to prove this if the nurse was on duty and working within the guidelines determined by the employer and profession. However, if the nurse is off duty the situation may be different because legally the nurse does not have a duty to intervene, although professionally, the NMC (2008) stipulates that the

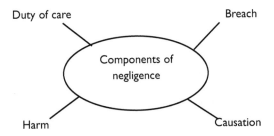

Figure 6.1. Components of negligence.

nurse has a professional duty at all times. In the case of, for example, a road accident, then the nurse takes on a legal duty to care for the person appropriately. Hence a duty of care would exist and the expectations of the nurse would be greater than that of the average passerby. Therefore, by attending to an accident victim, a duty of care exists and there is an expectation that the care provided will be of a reasonable standard, i.e. to the best of the nurse's ability.

Breach of duty of care

Rules and regulations are written to both guide and protect and they contribute to the standard of care that a patient may expect from a nurse in a given situation. You should now be aware of the origin of many of these rules and regulations which form professional guidelines, such as the NMC Code (2008).

There are also policies and procedures produced by employers that help determine the standards set, for example, manual handling or infection control policies. You may be able to recall statutory laws that relate to these, such as Health and Safety at Work Act (1974) and the Public Health (Control of Diseases) Act (1984). It is the practitioner's responsibility to find out what the standard is; ignorance is no defence in law.

Despite all this guidance, rules may be broken, either deliberately, when someone takes a 'short cut' perhaps, or unintentionally. In negligence terms, this is a breach in a duty of care. The claimant has to prove what standard of care was required and how it was breached. To assist in this the question of what is reasonable needs to be answered.

Activity

Legally, what does the word 'reasonable' imply?

45

The standard or precedence for reasonableness is known as the Bolam test which was set following the legal case of *Bolam v Friern Barnet HMC* [1957] (Dimond 2008, NMC 2008).

Bolam was a patient who was given electro-convulsive therapy (ECT). The practice at that time (1950s) did not usually involve giving a muscle relaxant or anaesthetic. As a result of the treatment, the plaintiff suffered fractures and sued the health authority. Bolam failed to obtain compensation because at the time, this was the accepted procedure and many other doctors in that field followed the same practice. In other words, this was the accepted standard of the day and the actions of the defendant were reasonable under those circumstances.

In the case of a nurse then, the test of reasonableness says that the standard is not that of the highest skilled nurse but of the ordinary skilled nurse who is practising that skill competently.

There have been other precedence cases such as *Whitehouse v Jordan* [1981] (Dimond, 2008) which have added to this question of what is reasonable. In *Whitehouse v. Jordan*, although there had been an error of judgement on the part of the obstetrician, he had been acting in a reasonable way.

These two cases highlight the fact that there may be differing bodies of opinion or sound reasons for not adhering to the accepted principles without being found negligent.

Was harm caused?

For a negligence case to be considered by a court the claimant must have been harmed in some way, unlike professional misconduct cases which do not have this requirement. The harm must also be the sort that is compensatable in law. This harm is often of a physical nature as it is easier to prove, but psychological or financial harm, such as loss or damage to property, may also be compensatable. In addition, the harm must be reasonably foreseeable due to the duty of care being breached.

For example, if a nurse assesses and records that a patient has a high risk of developing pressure sores and does not implement actions to prevent them it is probable that the patient will develop such sores. This failure to act is a breach of duty of care.

This example also illustrates the fourth component of negligence, i.e. causation (see *Figure 6.1*). The cause of the harm needs to be directly linked to the breach in the duty of care.

Consider the case of a seriously ill child who has meningitis. A doctor prescribes antibiotics but the dose he gives is 10 times the normal dose. The child becomes deaf. Was the doctor negligent, and was the harm caused because of the doctor's actions? It appears at first that this is a clear case of negligence as the doctor had a duty of care which he breached by giving an incorrect drug dose and the child suffered harm as a result. But was the deafness caused on balance of probabilities by the overdose of antibiotics? Meningitis is an infection that can result in deafness so it is not possible to conclude that it was the drug overdose alone that caused the harm, so negligence cannot be proven (*Kay v. Ayrshire and Arran Health Board* [1987] in Dimond 2008).

Sometimes the claimant does not know that any harm has been caused until many years after an event, such as in cases of asbestosis. Now the claimant has three years from the realisation of harm to sue for negligence. For example, a female patient has a sterilisation as a means of contraception and is told it will be impossible to conceive. She becomes pregnant several years later and it is at that time she realises the harm and can begin a claim for negligence.

You may think that more than one person was negligent in some of the following scenarios; identify them and explain how they could also have been negligent.

Activity

- Read the scenarios presented below, which are based on real negligence cases, to test your understanding. Use the four components that have to be proved by the claimant and decide for each:
- Who was negligent?
- How was their duty of care breached? Were the defendant's actions reasonable?
- What harm was caused? Was it foreseeable?
- Was causation directly a result of the breach of duty of care?

Scenario 1

In the cases *Wilsher v Essex Health Authority* [1986] and *Wilsher v Essex AHA* [1988] (Dimond 2008, McHale and Fox 2007) a premature baby required oxygen therapy in the neonatal unit. This needed careful and continuous monitoring of oxygen concentrations in the baby's blood via a probe inserted into a blood vessel.

A junior doctor inserted the probe into a vein instead of an artery. A senior doctor also made the same mistake. As a result, inaccurate oxygen levels were recorded. Because of this the baby was given too much oxygen by a nurse and suffered permanent damage to the retina of the eye and blindness.

- All three practitioners owed a duty of care to the baby and the baby did suffer harm.
- The nurse did not breach her duty of care because she administered oxygen based on the blood levels and could not have known that the doctors had incorrectly positioned the probe. Neither could the nurse be expected to recognise developing retinal damage as this was beyond her role and ability. She acted in a reasonable way.
- The junior doctor did not breach his duty of care because, although he inserted the probe incorrectly, he had asked his superior to check it. The junior doctor's actions were reasonable in asking for confirmation. The Bolam test applied.
- The senior doctor was found negligent because he breached his duty of care by failing to notice that the probe was in the wrong place. This resulted in harm to the baby which was foreseeable.

This case went to the House of Lords who held that the claimant had not proved that the excess oxygen had caused the blindness and they ordered a re-trial because of the issue of causation (Dimond 2008).

Scenario 2

In the case of *Maynard v West Midlands Regional Health Authority* [1984] (Dimond 2008, Pattison 2009) a patient presented at the hospital with symptoms of a chest complaint. The possible diagnosis included tuberculosis (TB); Hodgkin's disease, a potentially fatal disease if not treated early enough; and two other conditions. The doctor decided to perform an invasive procedure and biopsy to help determine which condition the woman had rather than wait for sputum results which would confirm TB.

The procedure carried a risk of damage to a nerve affecting the vocal chords and the patient sued because this did indeed occur. The results of the sputum test later showed a diagnosis of TB.

In this case the doctor had a duty of care but there were different expert medical opinions as to whether this was breached. Some experts stated that they would have gone ahead with the biopsy without waiting for the sputum results because of the severity of one possible diagnosis. Others would have waited rather than expose the patient to a procedure which carried risks.

Eventually, after appeal to the House of Lords, the original decision of negligence was overturned based on equally acceptable differences of opinion, both of which were reasonable in the circumstances. The House of Lords stated:

> *It was not sufficient to establish negligence for the claimant [sic] to show that there was a body of competent opinion that considered the decision had been wrong if there was also a body of equally competent professional opinion that supported the decision as having been reasonable in the circumstances.*
>
> Dimond 2008: 45

The burden of proof lay with the claimant who could not establish that the actions were unreasonable based on a balance of probabilities.

From these scenarios, you can see that there is much for the claimant to prove and opinions of other practitioners in the relevant field are sought to support the case. The question of what is reasonable is very important, along with the aspect of causation. Many cases first found on behalf of the claimant go to appeal or the House of Lords where the initial decision may be overturned. This is a very lengthy procedure, fraught with problems for the claimant who may choose to settle out of court.

It is important to emphasise that for the nurse, documentary evidence can play a crucial role in recalling events many years after the alleged negligence case has occurred.

Implications for the nurse

As students, practising under the supervision of a registered nurse, it should be almost impossible to be sued for negligence. However, if students knowingly collude with a registered nurse and do not follow recommended guidelines, policies and procedures they can find themselves answering a negligence claim in the civil court.

It is important that you keep up to date with current evidence and research, which is made widely available in nursing literature, and know what are the accepted standards of care.

You must ensure that your records are current, accurate and relevant. *Chapter 8* will look further at written communication.

Registered nurses should be aware of areas which have arisen in both professional discipline and negligence cases and be extra vigilant in these areas of practice.

References

Bolam v Friern Barnet HMC [1957] 2 All ER 118

Dimond B (2008) *Legal aspects of nursing* (5th edn). Longman, Harlow

Fletcher L, Buka P (2007) *A legal framework for caring* (3rd edn). Macmillan, Basingstoke

Kay v. Ayrshire and Arran Health Board [1987] 2 All ER 417

Maynard v West Midlands Regional Health Authority [1984] 1 WLR 634

McHale J, Fox M (2007) *Health care law* (2nd edn). Sweet and Maxwell, London

Moody M (2001) Why nurses end up in court. *Nursing Times* **97**(8): 24–6

Nursing and Midwifery Council (2008) *The Code: Standards of conduct, performance and ethics for nurses and midwives*. Nursing and Midwifery Council, London

Pattison D (2009) *Medical law and ethics* (2nd edn). Sweet and Maxwell, London

Whitehouse v Jordan [1981] 1 All ER 267

Wilsher v Essex Health Authority [1986] 3 All ER 801

Wilsher v Essex AHA [1988] QB 730, CA

Section 3

This section is very broadly entitled 'communication' since nurses spend a lot of time communicating. The title was chosen because it is reflected in the NMC's (2008) Code, and the NMC guidance on professional conduct for nursing and midwifery students (2010a) which highlights that good communication skills are vital.

When nurses communicate it is by word of mouth, non-verbally (body language) and by written means. Even these activities have legal, ethical and professional implications, as the two chapters in Section 3 demonstrate. *Chapter 7* focuses on the issues of truthfulness/truth-telling, choice, consent, autonomy and advocacy while *Chapter 8* looks at the many aspects of written communication.

To start with you need to think about a couple of situations to set the scene.

Activity

List situations when you might be asked to disclose personal information.

Your list of situations may contain items such as, in a bank or building society, a child's school, a doctor's surgery, or in offices that deal with tax, benefits or housing issues.

In addition, there are many places where people may be asked to give personal information about their health – accident and emergency departments, outpatients' departments and specialised clinics related to sexual or mental health issues.

Activity

- Think about the sort of environment that would encourage you to disclose personal information.
- What characteristics would you like the listener to demonstrate?

You would probably prefer an environment that is quiet, private and comfortable and where you will not be overheard. You will want the listener to be somebody you can trust, who is relaxed and attentive. When this person explains something, you will want them to talk in a language you understood. You will also not want to feel pressurised into revealing more than you wish. Other thoughts might include, what are 'they' going to do with this information?

CHAPTER 7

Principles of communication in different contexts

Rights, responsibilities/duties

For many years there has been discussion over 'patients' rights'. Different patients' charters have been written by the Department of Health to indicate the standards patients can expect when receiving healthcare. Statutory legislation, such as the Human Rights Act (1998), has set out a series of rights anyone can expect in life. Rights are often used as a means for individuals to get their own way. However, for every 'right' a person has there is also a 'duty' or 'responsibility'.

Cuthbert and Quallington (2008) discuss the links between these two complementary factors in an exploration of a rights-based approach to care. From a legal perspective Dimond (2008) highlights several areas where a patient has a legal right to:

- Healthcare (but not absolute).
- A reasonable standard of care.
- Give consent.
- Access health records.
- Confidentiality.
- Complain and have complaints dealt with speedily and effectively.

In addition, Thompson et al (2006) argue for the ethical right:

- to know
- to have privacy
- to treatment.

A statutory duty for NHS bodies under Health and Social Care Act 2001 requires that arrangements are made for consultation with people to whom services are provided (Montgomery 2003). To counterbalance their rights, patients also have responsibilities, such as giving as much information as they can to medical/nursing staff about their medical history, relevant family history and any treatment/medication.

To return to the list of patients' rights, not only do patients have responsibilities and duties corresponding to their rights, but nurses also have responsibilities and duties towards their patients.

Activity

Try to think of the duties/responsibilities a nurse has in response to patients' rights listed above.

Table 7.1. Patients' rights and nurses' duties/responsibilities	
Patients' rights	*Nurses' duties/responsibilities covered by the NMC*
A right to healthcare	Nurses have a legal and professional duty to care for patients
A right to a reasonable standard of care	Nurses must adhere to the standards in the NMC Code (NMC 2008)
A right to consent	Nurses must gain consent prior to any nursing procedure
A right of access to health records	Nurses must abide by the Data Protection Act 1998 and NMC guidelines
A right to confidentiality	Nurses must adhere to the NMC guidelines
A right to complain	Nurses need to apply the policies/procedures of the trust/organisation in which they work
A right to know (legal right)	Nurses need to give information honestly and truthfully (NMC 2008)
A right to privacy	Nurses need to respect the NMC standards (NMC 2008)
A right to treatment	Nurses have a duty to provide treatment whether active or palliative (Thompson et al 2006)

Table 7.1 may make it seem as if the nurse has no rights, however nurses do have rights, for example, if a nurse has suffered harm as a consequence of violence he or she can take action. According to Dimond (2008: 305), a nurse can:

• Sue the aggressor personally for trespass to the person.

- Sue the employer if the nurse can establish that there has been a breach of the employer's duty of care to them.
- Obtain compensation from the criminal courts following a successful prosecution of the assailant.
- Claim compensation from the Criminal Injuries Compensation Authority.
- Possibly receive, if eligible, statutory sick pay, Whitley Council sickness pay and social benefits.

The Health and Safety Executive publishes guidance about violence-related harm on its website (www.hse.gov.uk) and you might like to read it. Hopefully you will never be a victim of work-related violence, but by being familiar with the guidance you might be able to help a colleague.

Activity

Access the National Audit Office website and view the incidence of reported violence towards NHS staff. www.nao.org.uk

Another series of points that need to be mentioned here is outlined by Thompson et al (2006):

- Having rights does not mean that one is bound to exercise them.
- Having rights does not mean that their exercise is unlimited.
- Patients' negative rights are in general stronger than positive ones – that is the right to refuse treatment. If a treatment is subsequently given against the patient's will, it is technically criminal assault.

This leads the discussion to the key right of consent, which will now be explored.

Consent

A lot has been written on consent which covers legal, ethical and professional boundaries. This subject will now be explored from the nursing perspective, although it is fully acknowledged that nurses are not the sole custodians of consent. Issues will be raised that may have field-specific variations, so alternative methods of handling the differences will be discussed.

At the beginning of this chapter it was identified that when communicating there was a range of things that you would ideally want in place before divulging personal information. Hopefully this is how you might conduct an assessment interview with a patient on admission, or during your time with them. This is the time when you get to know about them and start to determine what they expect from their time in your care. You may determine how anxious they are, how much, if anything, they want to know about what is wrong with them and how ready they are to discuss implications of their disease process. All this has implications for the nurse when they ask a patient for their consent for a nursing procedure.

Activity
- Look at the following two definitions of consent and contrast them.
- Which definition would you prefer to be applied to you if you were receiving care or treatment?
- State why you made this choice.

- A voluntary decision made by a sufficiently competent or autonomous person, on the basis of adequate information or deliberation, to accept rather than reject some proposed course of action that will affect him or her (Gillon 1985).

or

- Individuals are entitled to sufficient knowledge about their condition and proposed treatment, with explanations of alternative treatments, to be able to make a rational decision regarding treatment choice and, subsequently, be capable of empowering physicians and healthcare workers to pursue a particular treatment offer (Brykczyńska 1989).

Both definitions contain elements that are expected before a decision is made by a patient. Competence/rationality is required by individuals giving consent and information needs to be given to them which will help them make a choice. The definitions differ on the outcome. Gillon (1985) states that after all the input, the person will accept rather than reject what is offered. Brykczyńska (1989), on the other hand, talks of alternatives and the patient taking the initiative to empower those who will provide the treatment/care.

Activity

- Locate the Department of Health (2009) *Reference guide to consent for examination or treatment* at www.dh.gov.uk. How is 'consent' defined within this document?
- Once 'consent' has been given, can patients then subsequently withdraw their consent and refuse the treatment/care?

There will be some people who, if they were the patient, would want to find out all about the treatment/care on offer but ultimately would trust the healthcare professionals to do the best for them. Others would want to know about the choices on offer, and would want to make their own choice. Another group would rather not know about what could go wrong or know the finer details of the proposed care and would prefer to trust the healthcare professionals. It is the trust the patient places with the healthcare professionals that forms the basis of consent; i.e. the person must already trust you in order to give consent (Cuthbert and Quallington 2008). When a nurse is assessing a patient there needs to be careful exploration of the amount of information the patient wants to hear so that when the time comes for a decision there are fewer things for the patient to worry about. Once the nurse has established the level of information required this detail must be clearly recorded in the nursing records. Another facet that the nurse must be aware of is the level of understanding that the patient has and his or her ability to make a rational decision. Nurses are not expected to complete a deep psychological analysis but should be aware of a person's competence to grasp any information given so that the approach taken is at an appropriate level. Factors that could hinder the understanding of information could include hearing impediments, the disease process itself, distractions or difficulty in understanding English.

All this is leading to the issue of when consent is required for the nurse to undertake a particular procedure. Refer back to the last activity box where you located the Department of Health's current guidance about consent; this document needs to be read in conjunction with the NMC Code (2008). Many of the points discussed in these documents will now be explored.

Activity

Read the Department of Health (2009) reference guide and the NMC code (2008) now to help you understand what follows.

Why is consent needed?

If a nurse approaches a patient and, without any positive indication on the part of the patient, carries out a procedure (however well intentioned) then the patient has the right to pursue legal action (Dimond 2008, Pattison 2009).

This could be trespass, which could lead to:

- A civil or criminal action for battery – if touched without permission.
- A civil action for assault – fear of being touched.

The information threshold for battery is, however, very low (Pattison 2009). To succeed in trespass, it has to be proven that there had been a real lack of consent by the patient, as demonstrated in the case *Chatterton v Gerson* [1981].

However, no battery is committed where the patient understands the broad nature of the treatment, even if this understanding is arrived at from accessing sources of information other than the nurse or other healthcare professional seeking consent. However, if a nurse or healthcare professional fails to explore the risks and implications of the treatment being proposed then the claim would be for negligence, not battery (Pattison 2009). Patients can only take an action for battery if:

- They are treated against their will (assuming the patient has the capacity to give consent).
- The patient receives a different treatment from the one he or she originally consented to.
- The consent was obtained by means of fraud.

The role of the nurse has advanced greatly, with many nurses making autonomous decisions about the diagnosis and subsequent treatment/care options for patients (such as the nurse performing an endoscope procedure for a patient); hence the nurse is required to have a basic understanding of the legislation related to consent when undertaking nurse-led procedures.

There are times when consent would not be required.

- *Life-threatening emergency*: This could be if a person has a cardiac arrest. Unless the patient had expressly stated that he or she did not want cardiopulmonary resuscitation (CPR) then it would be expected that CPR would be carried out if considered medically appropriate.

- *When a patient is sectioned under a relevant section of the Mental Health Act (1983 amended 2007)*: In this case medication can be given without consent. See later discussions.
- *Where public health is at risk under the Public Health (Control of Disease) Act 1984*: A patient may need to be isolated in a single room in hospital because of an infectious disease. Consent would be requested but could be overridden for the health needs of the majority.

How can a patient give consent?

Consent can be given:

- Expressly/explicitly
- Tacitly/implicitly
- Hypothetically.

Activity

Think of examples of these different ways of giving consent.

Expressly/explicitly

As the words imply, this type of consent gives a clear indication of agreement or approval. It can be in a written form or verbally by the patient saying, 'Yes', to getting out of a chair to be weighed. A simple nod of the head is also acceptable. It is becoming more widespread that nursing consent is gained in a written format. This is particularly so in nurse-led services; generally though nurses often have to deal with 'consent forms' that have been completed by medical staff. Nurses need to be aware of the importance of consent forms and these will be discussed further in *Chapter 8*.

Activity

Find and read the consent forms that are currently being used in your own area of practice so that you are familiar with the form your patient may ask you about in your role as their nurse advocate.

Tacitly/implicitly

It could be argued that any patient in a clinical/care provision setting has given his or her permission for any procedure to take place. This would be taking implied consent too far (McHale and Tingle 2001). Much more commonly, this type of consent can be seen in non-verbal communication. If you approach a patient with a syringe, and they are expecting to have an injection, then an arm or leg may be exposed for you to administer the injection. No words may have been spoken but the gesture is tacitly saying that you have that individual's consent.

Hypothetically

This type of consent is given in a, 'if such and such happens then...' context. There are two key types of hypothetical consent that a nurse will rarely gain, but may well have to act upon. These are when a person has an organ donor card or has written an 'advance directive' or 'living will'.

Who gains consent?

According to the Department of Health (2009) and the NMC (2008), the best person to seek consent is the person carrying out the treatment. There may be times when this can be delegated, but only if that person is both capable and specially trained.

When is consent needed?

Nurses are involved in many types of treatment and care where consent is required. Any procedure requires some form of consent and this is normally by agreement through nodding the head, saying yes, or offering the appropriate part of the body. Therefore, express/explicit, tacit/implied types of consent are used.

Depending on the type of clinical environment and trust protocols, written consent is required for some drug treatments such as chemotherapy and treatments under the Mental Health Act 1983. The latter requires agreement by a 'second opinion doctor'.

For all types of consent there must be validity.

What makes consent valid?

There are several factors that have to be adhered to. Consent must:

- Be voluntary: the individual must not be under sedation or manipulated into a situation of agreement.
- Be informed: the nature of the treatment, the risks involved, subsequent consequences and any alternatives must be given truthfully.
- Cover the act to be performed: if a patient has requested assistance with a bath, this does not mean that the nurse can also wash the patient's hair, cut his or her toe nails or trim his beard.
- Be from a legally competent source: there are laws and specific instructions that need to be adhered to, concerning who may give consent.

Who can give consent?

Adults
No adult can give consent on behalf of another adult if the latter is legally competent and has the capacity to make his or her own informed choice. However, the Mental Capacity Act 2005 does make provision for the appointment of a lasting power of attorney, and this individual can give consent on behalf of another (Dimond 2008). However, where no lasting power of attorney has been appointed by the patient there may be situations when the carers/relatives/friends are asked for their suggestions as to how the individual would normally react, but they cannot sign the consent form; consent needs to be given by the person concerned. A person, unless otherwise assessed, is considered to be mentally competent under Section 1(2) of the Mental Capacity Act 2005; the criteria to be used in assessing competence are set by Sections 2 and 3 of the Act (Dimond 2008).

Activity
Access the Mental Capacity Act 2005 at www.legislation.gov.uk, it would be beneficial for you to familiarise yourself with this piece of legislation. In particular, read Section 4 which refers to 'Best Interests'.

Minors
A parent, or someone to whom parental responsibility has been given, can give consent for treatment to a child. The law specifies the definition of consent and its boundaries.

According to the Family Law Reform Act (1969), for medical, surgical and dental purposes a child can give consent to treatment when aged 16. A later Act of

Parliament, the Children Act 1989 (as amended 2004) states that the wishes and feelings of the child should be ascertained and considered in the light of his or her age and understanding. This is obviously going to vary according to the child's mental age and experience.

Activity

Can you think of any situations when there might be a clash of wills over consent relating to a minor?

It was established in *Gillick v West Norfolk and Wisbech AHA* [1986] that a child under the age of 16 years can legally have the capacity to give consent to a medical examination and treatment (including contraceptive treatment) providing the child could demonstrate sufficient maturity and intelligence to understand the implications of what was consented to. The Gillick principle reflects the young person's transition from a child to adulthood. However, nurses need to be aware that under the Sexual Offences Act 2003, it is a criminal offence to procure sexual intercourse with a child under the age of 16 years. Thus, contraceptive treatment and advice should only be given on clinical grounds. Lord Fraser, in the Gillick case, issued guidelines (the Fraser Guidelines) to protect nurses from being accused of breaching the Sexual Offences Act 2003; these guidelines have been extended in section 13 of the Sexual Offences Act. This may mean not telling the child's parent(s) about the treatment if it is in the interest of the child's welfare not to do so.

Activity

Locate a copy of the Fraser Guidelines and read them.

Vulnerable patients

Included in this category are some elderly, mentally incapacitated or mentally ill people. A number of people may be mentally incapacitated for a short time due to sedation or unconsciousness.

There are many people who fall into this category of vulnerable adult. Overall, the principle that must be applied is that the best interests of the patient must be paramount. 'Best interests' goes wider than best medical interests and should include factors such as the individuality and wishes of the patient when they were competent (e.g. advance directive), their current wishes, their general well-being and their spiritual and religious welfare. According to Joyce (2007) 'best interest' does not reflect the personal views of the decision-maker, instead it requires an objective view on both the current and future interests of the person.

Trying to provide care in the best interests of the patient is not always easy. For example, relatives of older people, although they cannot formally give consent to treatment (unless they have a lasting power of attorney under the Mental Capacity Act 2005), can influence the care that is given. However, this may not always reflect the patient's wishes at that time. This could be because many older people are tired of living. When younger they may have undergone treatment to stay alive, but now they are ready to die. This does not imply that they would want to end their life, just not to prolong it. In this instance, non-intervention would be their choice if they were able to give their consent.

Activity

Using the legal perspective that has been outlined, think about the ethical and professional problems you might encounter in your area of practice. The reference list at the end of this chapter may help you.

With patients who are mentally incapacitated from any cause, then relatives, carers and friends may be able to give an indication of their wishes. However, there are some specific and clear guidelines issued by the NMC (2008) related to valid consent. The NMC Code (2008) states that nurses must be alert to and act upon indications that a vulnerable adult might be at risk of abuse. It is also recommended that the nurse should know which local policies to follow for guidance on vulnerable patients, as advocated by the NMC (2010b). The Department of Health's (2002a) guidance is recommended for nurses, particularly student nurses who may have had little experience of working with this group of society. The *Deprivation of Liberty Safeguards* (Department of Health 2007) came into effect in 2009 to safeguard those whose decision-making ability was incapacitated to ensure that their human rights are considered. In order to deprive an incapacitated patient of his or her liberty two health and social care professionals (including a mental health nurse) must assess the patient to ensure the proposed liberty deprivation is in the best interest of the patient. The patient can be detained for up to 12 months, however a review can be authorised earlier, and the patient is appointed an advocate. An assessment is also made to determine whether the patient would be better protected under a compulsory detention under the Mental Health Act 1983 (amended 2007).

The basis for valid consent is that it must be voluntary, informed, cover the act performed and be from a legally competent source.

When dealing with mental health patients, all the factors listed above apply, but there are other legal aspects a nurse must consider relating to the Mental Health Act 1983, the Mental Capacity Act 2005, and the Safeguarding Vulnerable Groups Act 2006 (which also encompasses the safeguarding of children in specific circumstances).

The Mental Health Act 1983 (amended 2007) identifies two groups of patients:

- Voluntary patients, i.e. those who have asked for treatment and are sometimes called 'informal' patients.
- Detained/sectioned patients who have complex mental health problems, may have no insight into their condition, and who are 'detained' for their own or the public's safety.

Following the Bournewood case (*L v Bournewood Community and Mental Health NHS Trust,* see Department of Health 1999) there is now another group recognised by the House of Lords. This consists of patients who are incapable of giving consent to admission to hospital and have not been detained under the Mental Health Act 1983. Staff have a duty of care to act in the patients' best interests under common law powers. However, even in the more recent legislation there is no clear legal definition under the Mental Capacity Act 2005 of 'best interest' (Joyce 2007, Dimond 2008). However, the Act does have a list of factors that must be checked for the assessment of a person's capacity. If patients are assessed under the Mental Capacity Act 2005 to lack the capacity to give valid consent, and if they do not have a lasting power of attorney appointed, they will be allocated an Independent Mental Capacity Advocate (IMCA) to represent their wishes.

The Mental Health Act 1983 was amended in 2007 to introduce the Independent Mental Health Advocacy Service (IMHAS). As with the IMCA, this advocate will work with the interest of the patient accessing mental health care. Consent should always be sought from mentally ill patients but there are some differences. Voluntary or informal patients can refuse to have treatment when asked for consent. This refusal must be respected unless there has been such a deterioration in their condition that they then fall into the second category and have to be detained under an appropriate section of the Mental Health Act 1983.

Common law powers to treat in the patient's best interests must be observed. The civil detention provisions under Part 2 of the Mental Health Act 1983, as amended, states there are legal requirements of mental healthcare providers when dealing with consent issues. Individuals who are detained under the Mental Health Act 1983 may be prescribed medication for their mental health condition. However, it is important that the nurse is familiar with sections 57, 58 and 59 to determine the particular legal definition of 'treatment'; these sections of the Act will also establish under which circumstances medication and electroconvulsive therapy (ECT) can be given to a patient sectioned under the Act. Correct forms and strict records must be kept of the patient's detention status and ability to consent.

Summary

This section has provided a brief overview of some pertinent legislation related to the concept of consent. However, you are advised to read around the subject areas in greater depth in order to develop a more comprehensive understanding of what constitutes valid consent.

You may have noticed that there is no law specifically on consent, but the issues arise from other areas of law.

A summary of the laws involved is shown in *Table 7.2*.

Table 7.2. Summary of laws involved in consent	
Field	*Legal source*
General principles	Trespass, assault, battery, negligence, common law principles
Mental health	Mental Health Act, Mental Capacity Act Safeguarding Vulnerable Groups Act
Child	Family Reform Act, Children Act
Learning disabilities	Children Act (if under 16 years), Mental Health Act, Mental Capacity Act, Safeguarding Vulnerable Groups Act

Activity
Look back to *Section 1* and check the name of the authors who outlined the five ethical principles. Now consider how these principles relate to this section.

Ethical and professional issues related to consent

One aspect of consent that has been mentioned but needs re-emphasising is that of informed consent – as Thompson et al (2006) stressed, the right to know. All patients, including those from any of the groups discussed above, need to have information about the choices they have to make. The choice may be to accept one or other option or refuse the treatment on offer. For the patient to be able to do this the information needs to be given truthfully but in a way that enables understanding, and at a rate that is acceptable to the individual. That is why the importance of individual assessment was highlighted at the beginning of this section. If the patient is to have autonomy, the choice that is given must not be one of 'take it or leave it' or 'Hobson's choice'. There needs to be a genuine choice and, as stated earlier, the consequences of each option need to be given.

The nurse's duty of care includes the duty to inform – see details on the Bolam Test with regards to negligence in Chapter 6.

This means that any breach is actionable, but only if harm can be proved. This contrasts with trespass, where harm does not have to be proved.

Truth-telling/truthfulness

From the activity on page 65 you should have been able to identify Thiroux and Krasemann (2007) as the authors of the principle of truth-telling (and of autonomy). Telling the truth is a value which is usually encouraged in early childhood. Thiroux and Krasemann (2007) endorse this, saying it is one of the hallmarks of true communication.

In 1999, Rumbold suggested the following activity; it is still useful.

Activity

Ask yourself whether you agree or disagree with the following statements:
- To tell the truth is right.
- One should tell the truth on all occasions.
- There are occasions when to tell a lie is justified.

You probably said that you agree with the first statement, but that you could argue for and against the other two.

The truth comes in many forms and sometimes the truth may not be suitable as it is too blunt and sounds uncaring. Does that mean a lie has to be told, or will you be 'economical' with the truth?

Think of some of the problems which could follow a lie. You will have to remember what you said for a start and then tell everyone else what you have said so that they can maintain the story. At a later date if you are somehow confronted with the lie, you may lose all trust and credibility.

Economy with the truth can also pose problems. You could easily be confronted with the fuller version of the truth and have to explain your actions, even if this may have been done to minimise harm (non-maleficence) to the patient. Whichever route you take there will be pitfalls.

By being sensitive to a patient's needs, there may be rare occasions when a person's condition might lead you to be selective (although never untruthful) about the information you give. How can a nurse tell the truth about a procedure? Consider this scenario:

Nurse: Hello Mr Grant, I've come with your suppositories.
Mr Grant: What are they for?
Nurse: You said you were very constipated. They help the bowel to work.
Mr Grant: How are you going to put them in?
Nurse: If you get on to your bed, turn on to your left side with your bottom near to the edge, then I will insert them having lubricated them first.
Mr Grant: Will it hurt?
Nurse: It may feel a little uncomfortable, so you need to try to relax.
Mr Grant: How quick do they work?
Nurse: You'll get some sensation to want to have your bowels open quite quickly, but you need to try to hold on for about 20 minutes for them to work properly.

On the face of it there is nothing wrong with the exchange between the nurse and Mr Grant, however:

- Did he have a choice?
- Was a choice necessary?
- Did the nurse outline any other consequences apart from success?

The possible need for immediate access to a toilet was not mentioned and the controversial 'truth' that 'if I insert these badly I could actually rupture your rectum' was not mentioned either.

What would you consider to be adequate as consent to this procedure?

This example may seem simple, but it does illustrate some of the points previously mentioned. Sometimes nurses have to face up to problems of truth-telling which are not of their making. The one which is often quoted is that of discussing diagnosis/prognosis with relatives without the patient's knowledge or vice versa.

An area where telling the truth can be difficult is if a patient refuses vital medication. There has been a lot of debate over this issue and court cases have followed when patients have been given medication in a disguised form. The NMC (2007) has issued guidelines if a patient is unable to give informed consent and the medication is in their best interests. Disguised medication must never be used for the healthcare team's convenience. In effect, the nurses are not telling the truth in their actions, but this may be seen as ethically the best course of action as the principle of least harm is being applied.

Truth-telling is only the first part of the process of giving information; after information has been given, then the patient has to make a choice. This is where autonomy comes in.

Autonomy

> **Activity**
>
> Find a definition of autonomy.

People have their individual differences, they have their own ways of being moral, and, as much as is possible, they follow the dictates of their own intelligence and conscience (Thiroux and Krasemann 2007). To do this they have to have an opportunity to choose. They also need sufficient information to make the choice (Fletcher and Buka 2007). The options put before patients should be in their best interests, and also set in the context of the 'common good' of the patients in that part of the wider health service (Thompson et al 2006).

When people in the healthcare setting have a choice they tend to follow one of four routes when confronted with needing to give consent to a procedure. These are:

- The patient can agree with the nurse and submit to the procedure.
- The patient may ask a lot of questions which the nurse must answer truthfully or, equally truthfully, acknowledge their limitations (NMC 2008) before a decision can be made.

- The patient may first agree to the procedure and then later refuse.
- The patient can refuse to have the procedure. This may be for a variety of reasons.

These are four ways of expressing personal freedom or autonomy.

At the beginning of *Chapter 7* we looked at two definitions of consent. Gillon (1985) assumed that, 'the patient would accept rather than reject some course of action that will affect him or her'. This is the assumption most of us (if we are truly honest) would make when asking for a patient's consent. How do we handle the situation when a person refuses outright, as in the medication example above? The easy answer would be to record 'drug refused' on the medication record.

Activity

What else needs to be considered when a patient is making a decision about consent?

The temptation, when patients refuse something that is offered and considered to be the best course of action, is to try to persuade them to change their mind (see Thompson et al 2006). This is sometimes described as 'paternalism' — the idea that we know best, so you must follow our instructions (Melia 2004). This does not allow for the patient's individual freedom. Having argued this, some people may say that to have a choice is very confusing, and that in fact healthcare professionals do know best (Tingle and Cribb 2007). It is one thing to stand in a supermarket and try to decide which brand of baked beans to buy but quite another to make a decision about surgery or drug therapy.

In the authors' experience, patients receiving verbal and nonverbal messages from staff can be subject to the following:

- Intense pressure to conform.
- Remarks which indicate the staff's displeasure.
- Ostracism.
- Reduced levels of care.

Unfortunately, sometimes staff do not know how to deal with the situation of rejection, they take it personally and respond accordingly. But if we believe it is a person's right to choose then we have to accept the person's right to refuse as well.

The care we give to that individual may change to accommodate the different care required, but the standard must be as high (NMC 2008).

Autonomy is not always possible. Many people do not have the capacity to choose. It is very important to create opportunities for autonomy and also to respect the autonomy an individual is capable of. Clearly, an infant, an unconscious patient and some people with learning disabilities and mental health problems will not be able to make an autonomous choice (Rumbold 1999).

When it is necessary to create autonomy, in certain circumstances this can be done by gently putting the situation back into patients' hands and giving them time to think about their decision. Often nurses are in such a hurry that there is little time for patients to deliberate and so they make the choice they think the nurse would like. Not everybody behaves in this way. There may be occasions when you might see your colleagues behaving in a less than helpful way towards patients who are exercising their autonomy. Such a situation might require you to undertake an additional role – that of advocate.

Advocacy

An advocate is one who pleads on behalf of another. Advocacy is about power: influencing those who have power for those who do not, particularly where a person lacks the capacity to make decisions (Dimond 2008).

Activity
In your everyday life, when might you act as an advocate for another?

Your answer may include speaking to a teacher on behalf of your child, acting as a go-between for friends who have quarrelled or signing a petition for or against something.

Advocacy is also a role that is used in the courts and that is why it is sometimes considered to be 'high powered'. It is a role that can be used effectively in the clinical setting to speak on behalf of one or a group of patients.

It must always be remembered that advocates plead for another person and express his or her wishes, not their own.

Activity
Think of situations when you have or might have to be an advocate for a patient.

The situation in which you may act as advocate will differ according to your area of nursing practice, but there will be similar themes.

- The patient is unable or unwilling to speak on behalf of him or herself.
- You have been one of a group who has campaigned for change, such as a change of time for a procedure.
- You defend a patient's decision by speaking to a colleague to explain it.

There will be some areas of advocacy which are relatively simple. The examples below follow no particular order:

- A patient does not know/understand information. This may be after a doctor has spoken to a patient about a procedure. Afterwards the patient asks you what it all meant. You are advised to recall the doctor to answer the patient's questions in a manner the patient can understand. Nurses may only answer questions within their level of knowledge (NMC 2008), otherwise they may be judged in a court of law if a complaint of negligence is made (see *Chapter 6*).
- A patient is incapable of making a decision.
- A patient cannot complete the daily menu sheet and you do it after discussion.
- An adult patient is asleep and has requested that he should not be disturbed; it is therefore not appropriate for a visitor to see the patient. The nurse acts as advocate for the patient when asking the visitor to return later. It is a request that may not be acceptable and the patient cannot ask for him or herself.
- Another example could be where a qualified children's nurse in the accident and emergency department discovers that the drug dose prescribed for a three-year-old is twice what it should be. Ethically it would not be in the child's best interest for the nurse to administer the drug, nor would it value the child's life. Professionally the nurse is accountable for her actions and would have to justify why she would give the large dose if she took that course of action. Legally the nurse could be sued for negligence if harm occurred to the child as a result of the drug overdose. To act as this child's advocate, the nurse needs to return the prescription sheet to the medical officer and ask for the dose to be checked and amended.

Other more complex areas of advocacy can be seen in *Figure 7.1*. These are all areas where a nurse may get involved. Each of these areas will now be discussed looking at the legal, ethical and professional implications for each.

Figure 7.1. Areas of advocacy.

Patient incapable of making a decision

This area of advocacy has been discussed under the section on consent. In all cases the best interests of the patient should be paramount.

Patient or visitor complaints

If a complaint is voiced, you should listen and not comment or act defensively. All NHS trusts have to have a policy for complaints (under the Hospital Complaints Procedure Act 1985, superseded by the National Health Service [Complaints]Amendment Regulations 2006, SI 2006 no. 2084; Dimond 2008) and the nurse acts as advocate by advising the complainant of the procedure to follow. Sometimes you may have to follow the complaint further if there is need for a report. You would then have to investigate or answer questions to establish whether there was cause for complaint. The outcome may be that you find yourself campaigning on behalf of the patient or relative, because you discover that there is a sound ethical reason for doing so, for example, it is the beneficent thing to do. The Patient Liaison Advocacy Service (PALS) has been part of the NHS since 2002, when it was launched by the Department of Health as part of the NHS Plan (Department of Health 2002b); PALS is a service that helps to provide relevant information for patients, and to support members of staff in their endeavour to help patients.

Patient abuse

Patient abuse can result in whistle-blowing if a member of staff is seen to be abusing a patient and misusing the privileged relationship a nurse has (NMC 2008). The Public Interest Disclosure Act (1998) gives protection to the whistle-blower as long as correct procedures have been followed (NMC 2010b).

Alternatively, you may see a relative abusing a patient and have to act as an advocate in a difficult situation. Again, it is important to remember that you are pleading on behalf of someone else and with his or her wishes.

Specific needs of vulnerable patient groups

The elderly, children, and those with learning disabilities and mental health problems are vulnerable in different ways. One common denominator is that they are often without power to deal with situations. Sometimes there will be group advocates who may have nothing to do with any healthcare professional. These include NSPCC, Age UK, Mind, and MENCAP. These organisations work on behalf of such patient groups on common problems although individual needs are also dealt with.

Relatives need help following a death

This situation will obviously depend on where you work. Many relatives need someone to act as an advocate when there has been a death. They may need someone to telephone to find out information which they cannot do in their state of grief.

Other relatives may find themselves in the position of making a decision about the harvesting of a loved one's organs to donate to another person. At this time, they need someone to act as a go-between so that they understand the process and do not feel too pressurised.

This may all sound very positive and a role which nurses would find satisfying. Unfortunately, this is not always so.

Problems of advocacy

There are various problems with advocacy (Melia 2004). It can:

- Cause disrupted relationships between colleagues from different disciplines.
- Lead a nurse to champion one patient but not another, leading to injustice.
- Be very time-consuming and therefore unpopular with the advocate, while also making the advocate unpopular as he or she may not be able to take an equal load of the work in a team.
- Cause conflict between the nurse's professional role and the interests/wishes of the patient.

Additional legislation and advocacy

Human Rights Act (1998)

There are a number of rights that human beings should have which are the founding principles of the Human Rights Act. These are listed by Dimond (2008) in an appendix where she also outlines the continuing effects of this law.

Public Interest Disclosure Act (1998)

This act has been introduced to protect those who, for whatever reason, have cause to 'whistle blow' in an organisation, provided they follow set protocols. This is obviously a great step forward from ostracism, dismissal and other negative responses individuals have encountered in the past when acting as an advocate.

Table 7.2 includes questions and actions an advocate may need to consider and their outcomes.

 This table demonstrates the legal, ethical and professional issues related to advocacy.

Table 7.2. Advocacy: Questions, actions and likely outcomes

Questions		
1. Is it legal?	• Yes, OK proceed • No, e.g. dying patient wants overdose of drugs – cannot proceed	
2. Is it ethical?	• Yes, OK proceed • No, e.g. relatives want you to be dishonest on their behalf – cannot proceed	
3. Is it professional?	• Yes, OK proceed • No, e.g. patient wants to give you a bribe for preferential treatment – cannot proceed	
4. What help is required?		
Actions		*Outcome*
Simple advocacy: No risk to advocate • education • explanation • encouragement • empowerment		Individual acts for him or herself
Intermediate advocacy: Some risk to advocate • speak to another on behalf of an individual • speak to another on behalf of a group • suggest alternatives • suspend action		Advocate acts for individual who may then act for him/ herself
Complicated advocacy: High risk to advocate • communicate widely: – whistle to blow? • challenge system • change practice • count cost – physical, emotional, professional		There may be some results of the action but this is often at personal cost

References

Brykczyńska G (ed) (1—9) *Ethics in paediatric nursing*. Chapman and Hall, London

Chatterton v Gerson [1981] 1AII ER 257

Cuthbert S, Quallington J (2008) *Values for care practice*. Reflect Press Ltd, Exeter

Department of Health (1999) *Health Service Circular HSC 1998/122 L v Bournewood Community and Mental Health NHS Trust Decision by the House of Lords in the*

Appeal. DoH, London

Department of Health (2002a) *No secrets: Guidance on developing and implementing multi-agency policies and procedures to protect vulnerable adults from abuse*. The Stationery Office, London

Department of Health (2002b) *The NHS Plan*. The Stationery Office, London

Department of Health (2007) *Deprivation of liberty safeguards and Mental Capacity Act 2005 local implementation networks*. The Stationery Office, London

Department of Health (2009) *Reference guide to consent for examination or treatment*. The Stationery Office, London

Dimond B (2008) *Legal aspects of nursing* (5th edn). Pearson Education, Harlow

Fletcher L, Buka P (2007) *A legal framework for caring* (3rd edn). Macmillan, Basingstoke

Gillick v West Norfolk and Wisbech AHA [1986] AC 112 (HL)

Gillon R (1985) *Philosophical medical ethics*. John Wiley, London

Joyce T (2007) *Best interests: Guidance on determining the best interests of adults who lack the capacity to make a decision (or decisions) for themselves [England and Wales]*. British Psychological Society, Leicester

McHale J, Tingle J (2001) *Law and medical ethics* (7th edn). Butterworth, London

Melia K (2004) *Health care ethics*. Sage Publications, London

Montgomery J (2003) *Health care law* (2nd edn). Oxford University Press, Oxford

Nursing and Midwifery Council (2007) *Standards for medicines management*. Nursing and Midwifery Council, London

Nursing and Midwifery Council (2008) *The Code: Standards of conduct, performance and ethics for nurses and midwives*. Nursing and Midwifery Council, London

Nursing and Midwifery Council (2010a) *Guidance on professional conduct for nursing and midwifery students* (2nd edn). Nursing and Midwifery Council, Lond on

Nursing and Midwifery Council (2010b) *Raising and escalating concerns: Guidance for nurses and midwives*. Nursing and Midwifery Council, London

Pattison D (2009) *Medical law and ethics* (2nd edn). Sweet and Maxwell, London

Rumbold G (1999) *Ethics in nursing practice* (3rd edn). Baillière Tindall, Edinburgh

Thiroux JP, Krasemann KW (2007) *Ethics: Theory and practice* (9th edn). Prentice Hall, New Jersey

Thompson IE, Melia KM, Boyd KM (2006) *Nursing ethics* (5th edn). Churchill Livingstone, Edinburgh

Tingle J, Cribb A (eds) (2007) *Nursing law and ethics* (3rd edn). Blackwell Science, Oxford

CHAPTER 8

Written communication

The final chapter of this book looks at the vital aspect of written communication. This is often derided by nurses as 'just a paper exercise' but it is a key area of nursing practice, as highlighted in the NMC's (2009) *Record keeping: Guidance for nurses and midwives,* and the NMC Code (2008).

There are numerous legal, ethical and professional issues surrounding written communication. The professional aspects are considered first. These include the types of written material and their importance and the role of the nurse in dealing with written records. Some of the laws that have influenced the professional guidelines are identified and legal implications for practice are outlined. Finally, a variety of ethical issues relating to records and record keeping are discussed as they affect the role of the student and the qualified nurse.

Professional aspects of documentation

The NMC (2009) highlights very clearly in the introduction to its specific guidelines on written communication that record keeping is an integral part of nursing and midwifery. Nurses and midwives are involved not only in handwritten documentation but also electronic record keeping which means they need to be computer literate in order to input patient information accurately.

Activity
- Make a list of all the different types of documents that you have to complete in your area of clinical practice.
- Consider who might use or read this documentation.

Your list might be very long, and your frustration at having to do so much paperwork might have been clear in your mind at the time you made your list.

Details commonly included in nursing records are shown in *Table 8.1.*

Table 8.1. Examples of nursing records	
Care plans	• Assessment sheets • Plans for specific care • Handwritten/electronic core care plans • Daily summaries of care given and reactions to this • Evaluations of care given and subsequent assessments
Charts for	• Fluid balance • Weight • Mood • Neurological observations • Nutritional intake • Blood pressure • Wound assessment, etc.
Records used by the multidisciplinary team (MDT)	• Accident/incident forms • Discharge letters/referral letters, consent forms • Prescription charts • Do not actively resuscitate (DNAR) forms • Single assessment documentation

Some records may well be used by all the people you have identified in the above activity, and, in addition, there are records that are held by the patient/ parent which are brought to the professional when relevant. These include antenatal records, child immunisation records and privately-funded records, such as X-rays and second opinions.

A vast number of people could, potentially, read any of these documents. In 1987, Siegler gave an example of a patient who asked how many people would read his documents and was told this was 75. Primarily records are written for professional staff who will be using them, e.g. nurses, midwives, medical staff, and professionals allied to medicine (PAMs), including pharmacists, occupational therapists, physiotherapists, speech therapists, radiographers, play specialists, social workers, etc.; the list is extensive. It must never be forgotten that the record is about an individual and that individual has the right to read his or her records. If records are needed for a court case related to any aspect of care then all the personnel involved in that case would be entitled to read relevant parts of the patient's records.

Due to the fact that people from different backgrounds will be reading the records, it is important that they are written in a format that will be understood by everyone. It is also much easier and safer to read a record that is in a logical and chronological order. It is important that all records are completed correctly. The NMC (2009) makes it clear that for records to be effective they must:

- Be factual, consistent and accurate.
- Be written as soon as possible after the event.
- Be clear and permanent and able to be photocopied.
- Be accurately dated, timed and signed, with the name printed by the first signature. A qualified nurse must countersign all records that a student completes.
- Be unambiguous, with any alterations crossed through, with the original still being legible. Alterations should be dated, timed and signed.

Records should not include abbreviations, jargon, meaningless phrases, irrelevant speculation or offensive subjective statements.

- *Abbreviations*: These are commonly used in nursing. Many trusts have a list of approved abbreviations for you to use. Any other abbreviation must be written in full the first time they are used, followed by the abbreviation in brackets.
- *Jargon*: This is commonplace in nursing but it needs to be explained to the patient verbally or an explanation written in the records.
- *Meaningless phrases*: Usually these are a combination of the above.
- *Irrelevant speculation*: 'This patient will come to a sticky end' is really rather unhelpful.
- *Offensive subjective statements*: No statement in a record should be offensive. A subjective statement is one that is based on your own biased opinion. An objective statement is one where specific facts are included, for example, 'Mabel has had a home visit today and says she is feeling very tired'.

Records should be written in conjunction with the patient/carer and written so that the latter can understand the content. Entries need to be consecutive, with clear evidence that care has been planned on the basis of assessment, then implemented and subsequently evaluated.

An example of a record that should never have been written is shown in *Figure 8.1*.

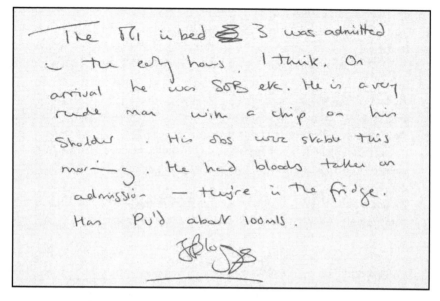

The bed 3 was admitted in the early hours, I think. On arrival he was SOB etc. He is a very rude man with a chip on his Sholder. His obs were stable this morning. He had bloods taken on admission — they're in the fridge. Has PU'd about 100mls.

Figure 8.1. Example of a poorly written record.

This record was written in pencil and the student's signature was written over white erasing fluid.

> **Activity**
>
> Using the NMC's checklist above, identify which of the NMC (2009) guidelines for record keeping have been ignored.

- The record is not factual or accurate, e.g. 'I think', 'obs were stable'.
- It is not dated or timed, therefore, is it current? Was it written as soon after the events as possible?
- It is in pencil; anything could be erased and accuracy could be questioned. It is also not suitable for photocopying.
- Additions have been made and there are no correcting signatures, nor has a qualified nurse countersigned the record. It is unclear who made the record and his or her status.
- It contains so many abbreviations, jargon words and meaningless phrases that the record would be difficult for a patient to understand and would be ridiculed in a court of law. (Please see the section on legal issues on page 83

to understand why the patient needs to understand the record.)
* There is a very derogatory sentence in this report that should not be there. What right has the writer of the report to make a judgement on a man who has been admitted in pain following a myocardial infarction?

Discussion points

* Think about the abbreviations

    e.g. SOB — how many things can this abbreviation stand for? Shortness of breath, sat out of bed, an American expletive.
* What do you think the 'etc.', in the record might mean?

    It could be that Fred was in pain or that he was suffering all the attendant physical symptoms a person with a 'heart attack' might have.
* PU'd is a terrible abbreviation of passed urine, but is often used.

Points to consider

It is important to write records or complete forms as soon as possible after the event. It is difficult to remember precise details after time has elapsed and you may have done a variety of other things in between, even if you know you have got to remember the details.

Another point to remember is that one word could convey different sets of circumstances. For example, the words 'slipped' and 'fell' could both mean an individual was once upright and then horizontal. The reason could be because of something external (slipped on a spilt substance), or internal (fell due to a change in blood pressure). The consequences if a court case ensued could be very different.

Nursing records

The admission sheet contains all the personal details of the patient and his or her baseline observations. The assessment sheet contains information about the patient's needs within a model of nursing. The care plan identifies the way the nurses will be caring for the patient. In the case of the patient in *Figure 8.1* this would include issues such as pain management, intake and output, and any special pressure-relieving instructions. Such a patient may also be very anxious about himself and his home circumstances and this needs to be explored and possibly a referral made for additional support from someone like a social worker.

Additional records

> **Activity**
> - Think of other records that might be included in this man's nursing records.
> - Items such as prescription sheet, fluid balance chart, pressure sore indicator, record and pain assessment chart could be included.

So far the writing of records has been clearly identified as part of the nurse's role.

> **Activity**
> - What other responsibilities does a nurse have with regard to records and record keeping?
> - As well as fulfilling the NMC's guidelines for the writing of records, the nurse's role extends further than completing the writing element already discussed.

Figure 8.2 identifies the many facets to the nurse's role within record keeping.

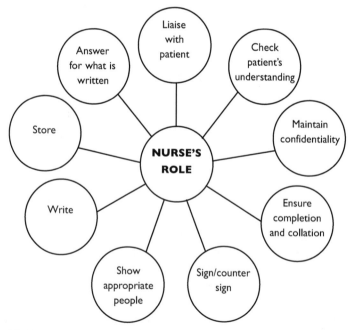

Figure 8.2. Facets to the nurse's role within record keeping.

Legal aspects of written communication

The two main areas of law covered here concern confidentiality of written communication and how and when this may be breached, and the security, protection and access of data. You have already discovered that numerous people are likely to be involved in healthcare delivery and that, if as many as 75 people could legitimately need to know something about a patient to provide continuing care, how can confidentiality ever be maintained? The principles of confidentiality apply to both verbal and written information which may be in a manual and/or computerised form, but the emphasis here will be on written communication.

The law recognises that confidentiality is not absolute (Dimond 2008); nursing records may be required by a court as evidence in negligence cases, for example. In addition, the Audit Commission studies records within hospitals and makes recommendations for improvement of the quality of such records to help defend negligence claims. Courts take the view that if an action has not been recorded it has not been performed (NMC 2009).

Confidentiality is closely associated with negligence and forms part of the duty of care of the health professional, including nurses. A legal duty exists in both common law and statutory law to maintain confidentiality. Disclosure of written information, without patient consent, is only allowed in certain circumstances.

The Human Rights Act 1998 (Schedule 1, Part 1) also imposes a statutory 'right to respect for private and family life' and that exceptions should only occur when required by law under specific situations (Dimond 2008: 17).

In many situations, if asked, patients will give consent to disclosure and sharing of written records which will enhance their care and treatment without recourse to the law. Without the consent of the patient, there may be justifiable reasons to breach confidentiality when it is in the patient's best interests, for example, to prevent harm occurring to the patient (Dimond 2008). These circumstances are closely linked to the professional and ethical reasons discussed elsewhere in this chapter. Where information is required about a patient, but consent has not been given, or the patient is incapacitated and cannot give consent, then Section 60 of the Health and Social Care Act 2001 (now Section 251 of the NHS Act 2006) enable the use of confidential information without breaking the law.

Caldicott guardians

The arrangements for using and sharing patient-based information within each NHS organisation is overseen by a guardian. If patient-identifiable information has to be shared, the guardian ensures that this is for a justifiable purpose, with only the minimum necessary information released.

Activity

Access a copy of the Caldicott Report to establish its key principles in relation to the release of patient-identifiable information.

Legally, there are instances when disclosure is compulsory. The Acts concerned include:

- *The Road Traffic Act 1988* where details have to be given to the police if personal injuries or death occur.
- *Prevention of Terrorism Act 1989/Anti-Terrorism, Crime and Security Act 2001* where injuries occur which may be a result of terrorist activities and there is reason to believe that an act has taken place or is likely to take place.
- *Public Health (Control of Disease) Act 1984* requires personal details to be provided to the district medical officer where notifiable diseases, such as cholera, smallpox, typhus or food poisoning, are suspected.
- *Police and Criminal Evidence Act 1984* enables the police to apply for powers via a judge to obtain access to material that is otherwise excluded from this legislation, such as personal records, which are confidential.
- *Abortion Act 1967* requires doctors to inform the Chief Medical Officer or the Department of Health about the termination of pregnancy.

Powers of the court

Additionally, a court has the power to order documentary evidence to be provided as well as requiring a healthcare professional to attend as a witness. This is known as a subpoena and it is in the interests of justice. There are some exceptions to these powers, which include issues of national security or legal privilege. However, legal privilege does not extend to nurses.

Public interest

Breach of confidentiality may be justified if it is in the public interest, defined as the interests of an individual, groups of people or society as a whole (NMC 2008).

A serious crime may be suspected, for example rape or child abuse, or an individual or groups of individuals may be at risk if someone else's health problem is not revealed. Dimond (2008) discusses the problems of public interest as there is very little guidance from the courts, apart from the American case of *Tarasoff v Regents of University of California* in 1976, and *W v Edgell* [1990]. In this latter case, an independent psychiatric report was passed to the Medical Director of W's hospital and a copy was forwarded to the Home Secretary. The psychiatrist believed the Home Office should be aware of the patient's mental health state.

This is just a brief summary of some of the legal issues surrounding confidentiality and it is unlikely that any individual nurse will be required to make decisions in relation to them alone. The onus for decision making is more often on the doctor. Other members of the healthcare team, including nurses, may either be the first to be aware of potential conflicts or be party to the decision to breach confidentiality. Of course, the nurse has to deal with the patient and the consequences of such breaches in a professional and sensitive manner.

There is also legislation that relates to security of, and access to information. The main acts are summarised below and you are asked to think about some of the implications for nurses.

Computer Misuse Act 1990

This broad act aims to combat various forms of deliberate misuse (including 'hacking') which are of public concern. As there is increasing use being made of computerised record systems in all areas of healthcare, the nurse needs to know the key aspects.

The main offences are:

- Unauthorised access or intent to access, or to make a computer perform a function, which may enable access to an unauthorised person.
- Helping someone else commit an offence.
- Unauthorised modification of contents which may impair computer operation, prevent/hinder access to data or impair the reliability of data.

In other words, this means a deliberate attempt to do something that affects the way a computer works or changes something the computer has recorded so that it affects the information it contains in some way.

If any of these offences are committed and the person is found guilty, a six-month prison sentence and/or fine may be imposed.

This sounds very technical and worrying for those dealing with computerised data, but the purpose is to protect individuals who have confidential information stored on computers. Nurses must ensure that their practice does not allow anyone without appropriate permission to have access to a patient's personal information.

> **Activity**
> Find out how this is safeguarded in clinical practice.

Access to Medical Reports Act 1988

This legislation enables patients to access medical reports written for insurance or employment purposes. The patient must be told a report is being asked for, give permission and be given the opportunity to see it before it is submitted. If anything is incorrect the patient is allowed to amend the report. There are some exceptions to safeguard the patient (Dimond 2008).

> **Activity**
> How might the Medical Reports Act apply to you?

Data Protection Act 1998

This law is an amalgamation of the previous 1984 Data Protection Act and the Access to Health Records Act 1990, most of which it replaces. Like the Computer Misuse Act 1990 it aims to protect individuals from the misuse of personal information (Hendrick 2000: 106). The act sets a similar standard to that determined by the NMC (2009) guidelines in that, for example, data should be accurate, secure and confidential.

Under the Data Protection Act patients can now apply to see both computerised and hand written information about them irrespective of how far back the record was made. Earlier legislation restricted manual record access to records written after 1 November 1991.

Access is requested in writing by the patient to the person who either made the record or, in the case of an institution, such as a hospital, to the data controller who consults with the professional who made the record. A maximum £50.00 fee can be charged.

> **Activity**
> - List what you think could be the reasons for access.
> - Inspection, explanation, copy, correction are some suggestions to help you.

Access applies to the patient, a person with written authorisation, a person having responsibility for a child (where the patient is the child), or a person appointed by the court (for incompetent patients).

Access is not absolute as it can be denied or restricted if there is a risk of physical or mental harm to patients as a result of letting them see their records. There are also restrictions imposed if another person mentioned in the record refuses consent or may be harmed as a result of disclosure (Dimond 2008). Under the Freedom of Information Act (2000) members of the public can also access information held about them by public authorities (Dimond 2008).

> **Activity**
> Make some notes on the implications of the Data Protection Act for the nurse. Identify some specific types of situations which you think could arise where access might be denied.

As mentioned earlier, record keeping often comes under scrutiny in negligence cases and patient complaints. Most problems occur through failure in basic communication, such as poor record keeping and not passing on enough information. Nurses should develop more reflective practice and keep up-to-date by reading professional literature to help heighten awareness of recurring problems.

Ethical aspects of written communication

Thiroux and Krasemann's (2007) principles relating to ethics were discussed in Section 1. These will now be related to written records and the example of poor handwritten record keeping in *Figure 8.1*.

Value of life

The record in *Figure 8.1* did not demonstrate that the nurse valued the patient's life. He was considered a rude man who had a chip on his shoulder. If people are anxious, they often come across as being rude, and a nurse needs to remember this and not make unwise judgements. By labelling a patient, the nurse removes that person's individuality.

Another example of demonstrating this principle is if you correctly collate documents for certain procedures, e.g. prior to surgery, when mental health rights have to be checked, or when social services discussions have to be processed.

When using a patient's records the nurse must maintain the confidentiality of the contents. For students who are writing case studies or reflecting on critical incidents, it is important to gain the consent of the person but still change all the details. By doing this, you are respecting that individual and recognising that they do not want private information shared with others.

Goodness or rightness

Records are written and maintained for the continuity of care for an individual. This is why they always need to be accurate and clear so that subsequent readers can do the most good for a patient (beneficence). It would be unethical to show a record (which would contain personal information) to anyone who asked. There is always a need to check on the individual's 'need to know'. The notion of confidentiality is based on this principle.

Confidentiality is an ethical issue as well as a legal one. Records generally need to be seen by a large number of people and it is vital that a person's trust in the healthcare team is not destroyed by the breaching of confidentiality. However, there are some circumstances where a breach of confidentiality is permitted, but this would need to be following heart-searching and discussions with relevant personnel. Ideally disclosures should only be made with the patient's consent, however disclosure can also be made by order of the court or where you can justify disclosure in the wider public's interest. See the section on legal aspects of communication earlier in the chapter.

Truth-telling and honesty

Truth-telling and honesty are highly relevant. When writing records it is essential to tell the truth and use the most appropriate words. Look back at page 81 where the two words, slipped and fell were used, and consider the consequences of using the wrong words.

Activity

Think of another example where similar words could convey different meanings.

In the truth-telling context you need to make sure that patients understand what is happening or is going to happen to them and the possible consequences of the procedure. If patients are unsure, the NMC (2008) advises that you tell other members of the healthcare team that this is the case, and also act as advocate by arranging for the appropriate person to come and discuss the situation with the patient. It is imperative that an honest record is made of any discussion.

By signing or countersigning a document you are saying, 'This is true'. Always read what you are going to sign to make sure that is the case. Do not forget that records may be required in a court of law or for professional misconduct cases.

Justice and fairness

It is in patients' best interests that they have the option to contribute to the care that they receive and it is only fair that they can have the opportunity to see documents and have these explained to them. This has been discussed in the legal aspects of communication part of this chapter.

Autonomy, individual freedom

All the examples given above which relate to patients being involved in their records and the keeping of their records, imply that there is the opportunity for choice. The patient may choose to let professional staff advise them rather than to question them. The patient's wishes must be honoured.

You will also need to consider the patient's autonomy when writing records as the patient can challenge what you have written and then you will have to justify your actions, in other words, be accountable. In some circumstances, a patient may personally contribute to the records. For example, by completing a fluid balance chart.

Activity

Think of other examples where you give patients the responsibility for an aspect of their records.

This chapter concludes with a quiz to consolidate the lega, ethical and professional aspects of written communication followed by useful facts about records and record keeping.

Quiz
1. Why do nurses need to keep records?
2. How should a record be presented? (content and style)
3. Who owns a patient record?
4. Make a list of people who have right of access to records.
5. For how long should a record be retained?
6. Why is this timescale set?
7. Name and date some specific laws that relate to health records.
8. Give a summary of each.
9. Under what circumstances can a patient be refused access to his/her own records?
10. Find a definition of confidentiality.
11. Give specific reasons why and when confidentiality may be breached.
12. Using drug administration documents as a focus, identify some of the associated record-keeping pitfalls.
13. Which NMC documents give help and advice to nurses regarding records?
14. Suggest which of Thiroux and Krasemann's ethical principles might relate to records and record keeping, and why.
15. What are the qualified nurse's responsibilities towards a student when the latter is completing a patient's/patient's record?

Useful facts about records and record keeping

Sometimes it is easier to remember facts if they are put in an unusual format. Using the alphabet, here are some facts to remember about records and record keeping:

A   Nurses are **A**ccountable for the patient's records and should **A**void **A**bbreviations.
B   Must be written in **B**lack ink.
C   Must be **C**orrect, **C**urrent, **C**omprehensive, **C**hronological, **C**onsistent, **C**ountersigned, **C**onfidential, and **C**omputerised.
D   Should be **D**etailed and **D**ated.
E   Can be used as **E**vidence.
F   Must be written **F**actually.
G   Can be **G**iven to the patient under the Data Protection Act (1998).
H   Must be **H**onest; and legible when **H**and written.
I   Must **I**nvolve patient, carers and significant others.
J   Must be **J**udgement free.
K   Need to be **K**ept for varying periods of time, e.g. adults and children.
L   Need to be **L**egible and **L**iterate and are a **L**egal requirement.
M   Should be **M**eaningful and useful to the **M**ultidisciplinary personnel who read them.
N   **N**o-one should make any derogatory comments.
O   Should be **O**bjective.
P   Suitable for **P**hotocopying.
Q   Should **Q**uestion your practice for improvements when necessary.
R   Demonstrate your **R**ationale for care delivery.
S   Must be **S**igned.
T   Must be **T**imed and dated.
U   Should be **U**naltered.
V   Should be **V**erifiable and **V**alid.
W   'If it has not been **W**ritten (recorded) it has not been done.'
X   No mistakes, but if there are, they need to be crossed through and signed.
Y   Always ask, 'Why am I writing this record?' 'Who is going to read it?'
Z   Be **Z**ealous for excellence.

References

Dimond B (2008) *Legal aspects of nursing* (5th edn). Longman, Harlow

Hendrick J (2000) *Law and ethics in nursing and health care*. Stanley Thornes, Cheltenham

Nursing and Midwifery Council (2008) *The Code: Standards of conduct, performance and ethics for nurses and midwives*. Nursing and Midwifery Council, London

Nursing and Midwifery Council (2009) *Record keeping: Guidance for nurses and midwives*. Nursing and Midwifery Council, London

Siegler M (1987) cited in: McHale J, Tingle J, Peysner J (1998) *Law and nursing*. Butterworth-Heinemann, Oxford

Tarasoff v Regents of University of California 17 Cal 3d 425 (1976) (USA)

Thiroux J, Krasemann KW (2007) *Ethics: Theory and practice* (9th edn). Prentice Hall, New Jersey

W v Edgell [1990] 1 All ER 835 and 1 All ER 855CA

Additional reading

Banks S, Gallagher A (2009) *Ethics in professional life*. Palgrave Macmillan, Basingstoke

Beauchamp L, Childress F (2001) *Principles of Biomedical Ethics*. 5th edn. Oxford University Press, Oxford

Department of Health (2003) *Confidentiality: NHS code of practice*. Department of Health, London

Department of Health (2003) *The Victoria Climbié Inquiry* (Lord Laming CM 5730). The Stationery Office, London

McHale J, Tingle J (2007) *Law and Nursing*. 2nd edn. Elsevier, Canada

Robinson S (2008) *Spirituality, ethics and care*. Jessica Kingsley Publishers, London

Websites

Action on Elder Abuse: *www.elderabuse.co.uk*

Age UK: *www.ageuk.org.uk*

Audit Commission: *www.audit-commission.gov.uk*

British and Irish Legal Information Institute: *www.bailii.org*

Carers UK: *www.carersuk.org*

Care Quality Commission: *www.cqc.org.uk*

Department for Children, Schools and Families (Children Act 2004 guidance):
www.dcsf.gov.uk/everychildmatters

Department of Education: Safeguarding and Social Work Reform guidelines:
www.education.gov.uk

Department of Health: *www.dh.gov.uk*

General Medical Council: *www.gmc-uk.org*

Health and Safety Executive: *www.hse.gov.uk*

HM Courts Service: *www.hmcourts-service.gov.uk*

Independent Safeguarding Authority: *www.isa-gov.org.uk/*

Legislation – Government legislation: *www.legislation.gov.uk*

Medical Protection Society has good advice about gaining consent from children
www.medicalprotection.org

MENCAP (learning disabilities charity): *www.mencap.org.uk*

Mind (mental health charity): *www.mind.org.uk*

National Audit Office: *www.nao.org.uk*

NHS Evidence- has a large data base of standards and guidelines: *www.library.nhs.uk*

NHS Litigation Authority: *www.nhsla.com*

Nursing and Midwifery Council: *www.nmc-uk.org/*

National Society for the Prevention of Cruelty to Children: *www.nspcc.org.uk*

Scottish Government: *www.scotland.gov.uk*Appendix

Appendix

The following questions may help you to pull together many of the strands that have been identified in this book. They are designed to help you to consider the different issues that have been presented and hopefully will help you see how the legal, ethical and professional issues affect your day-to-day practice as a nurse, whether you are a student or qualified.

Question 1

Using the NMC Code (NMC 2008), the *Record keeping: Guidelines for nurses and midwives* (NMC 2009) and the concept of confidentiality discuss the legal, ethical and professional issues a student nurse should consider when making an entry in a patient record.

Question 2

Consent, truth-telling and autonomy are vital factors to consider when undertaking patient care. Discuss the legal, ethical and professional implications of these factors when you are delivering care to a patient in your area of practice.

References

Nursing and Midwifery Council (2008) *The Code: Standards of conduct, performance and ethics for nurses and midwives*. Nursing and Midwifery Council, London

Nursing and Midwifery Council (2009) *Record keeping: Guidelines for nurses and midwives*. Nursing and Midwifery Council, London

Index